Race Your Best

A Plethora of P's for Phenomenal Performance

Doug Stutz
Master of Sport Science
United States Sports Academy

Stutz, Doug, 1961-
  Race Your Best: A Plethora of P's for Phenomenal Performance
    / S. Douglas Stutz

ISBN 978-1-4116-9659-4 (soft cover)
1. Running. 2. Running—Racing

First Edition, 2006

Cover design by Dylan Todd & Bryan Swain (Photo by Michael Lewis).

Praise for
Race Your Best:
A Plethora of P's for Phenomenal Performance

"As a runner, Doug Stutz developed his ordinary talent to do extraordinary things. He has made a career of mentoring others to not only shoot for the stars, but to reach them. The principles espoused in *Race Your Best* are universal. Apply them to your own situation to realize greater, more consistent success."
Ed Eyestone, *men's cross-country head coach at Brigham Young University. 1984 NCAA cross-country champion and two-time U.S. Olympic marathoner. Runner's World columnist.*

"Doug Stutz is one of the great leaders in our sport and one of the great leaders in this country! Anyone can teach a young man or woman the physiology involved in running fast. But it takes much more to teach them how to be a champion! Doug Stutz is a champion! For years he's taught young men and young women how to be champions, on the track and in life! And now, in *Race Your Best*, he's sharing that knowledge with all of us!"
Dave Barney, *men's and women's cross-country and track head coach at Paradise Valley Community College in Phoenix, AZ, the 2004 NJCAA women's and men's national champions in cross-country.*

"Coach Stutz has discovered the principles that enable an athlete to develop, focus and execute a plan. As a professional track and field athlete for 12 years, eventually I learned the same principles. Learning and applying these principles will benefit every distance runner in every aspect of running, both training and racing. Had I had access to these principles early on in my career, especially with Coach Stutz's creative presentation, my running would have benefitted greatly, especially as I was learning."
Doug Padilla, *track & field operations director at Brigham Young University. Set seven American Records at distances from 3000 meters to 5000 meters. Veteran of five World Championships and two Olympic Games.*

"I found *Race Your Best* very interesting! Readable and with a very strong human element to each section, it is very motivational material...yet written in a way that provokes the runner to think about the many things that goes through his/her mind when training and racing. I find that a big stumbling block with athletes is in gaining confidence as a runner. *Race Your Best* gives them usable information to help with this. I found the material a breath of fresh air! Many of the books on distance running are focused on the physiology of what goes on. This approach deals with most everything else, and of course it is these things that are the athlete's reality when training and racing. I think any runner would benefit from reading this!"

Will Freeman, *men's cross-country and track head coach at Grinnell College in Iowa. Former chair of the USA Track & Field coaching education program. Co-author of* High-Performance Training for Track and Field.

"As a coach of young developing athletes, I am always searching for ways to teach and prepare my athletes to perform their best. *Race Your Best* with its plethora of P's has really simplified many of the philosophies and concepts I try to instill in my runners. It has given me a creative and memorable way to introduce and teach these principles so they can remember and implement them into our program. Many of my runners have read and often refer to points they discovered that have helped them. This book is an easy yet informative read, and one I would recommend."

Brett Hill, *boys' and girls' cross-country and track head coach at Firth High School in Idaho. Has coached 21 State Championship teams and 47 individual State Champions in cross-country and track since 1994.*

Table of Contents

Post-Race P's

Foreword

I first met Doug Stutz when we were both students at Brigham Young University. I had returned a year earlier from a mission to El Salvador, and he was a freshman, preparing to leave on a mission. He was ready to work and eager to learn. We both were living on-campus in Deseret Towers. Under the direction of BYU distance coach Sherald James, the team looked like it would be strong. I was a returning All-American. Ed Eyestone and Lin Whatcott were among the promising newcomers.

We worked hard that year. I sprained an ankle in the middle of the season and lost two weeks training. Doug's strength and confidence increased as our training matched the preparation necessary to be competitive. He surprised a lot of people by finishing among the team's top seven most of the season. At the end of the year, Doug turned in his mission papers and received a call to serve in Argentina.

Doug returned from his mission with a renewed desire, eventually working his way back into shape and onto the team. By the time of his senior year in 1985, he was one of the team leaders. In most of the meets he was finishing as the top BYU runner.

After BYU Doug attended the United States Sports Academy, where he earned a master's degree in 1987. Equipped with the credentials, he became an assistant track coach at Ricks College in Rexburg, Idaho. In 1992 he was named head cross country coach for both the men and the women. Little did the athletic department know at that time that they would soon witness the establishment of a dynasty!

Before Coach Stutz would retire in 2001, the Ricks College Vikings would become the dominant men's and women's NJCAA cross country teams in the nation. Coach Stutz and his athletes won ten national championships, three in a row for the men (1999, 2000, 2001) and seven in a row for the women (1995-2001). He coached five athletes to individual cross-country national championships: Men (Jeff Davidson, 2000); Women (Kara Ormond, 1996; Alycia Boyer, 98; Kristen Ogden, 00;

Angela Benson, 01). Doug had similar success on the track. As an assistant track coach he coached four athletes to NJCAA individual national championships: Women (Cindy Reeder, 1500m, 1990; Holly Peterson, 10000m, 1996, 97; Melanie Clark, 800m, 1997; Alycia Boyer, 10000m, 1998). He was named head track coach in 2000 where he coached his athletes to six more NJCAA individual national championships: Men (David Woodbury, 10,000m, 2002; Ryan Griffeth, 3000m Steeplechase, 2002); Women (Angela Benson, 3000m Steeplechase, 4x800m Relay, 2002; Andrea Chugg, 4x800m Relay, 2002; Lida Clapier, 4x800m Relay, 2002; Sarah Dimmick, 4x800m Relay, 2002).

How could a coach have such an impact on his athletes as to almost uniformly empower them to achieve such great heights? This book answers this question. As an athlete and as a coach, Coach Stutz has discovered the principles that enable an athlete to develop, focus and execute a plan. His athletes learn to prepare themselves; they learn to believe in themselves; and, they learn to execute an effective race strategy. Yet, perhaps most importantly, Coach Stutz has developed a simple, yet very effective method of teaching these principles to his athletes, tools that benefit each athlete at the exact moment when they find themselves in need.

As a professional track and field athlete for 12 years, eventually I learned the same principles. Learning and applying these principles will benefit every distance runner in every aspect of running, both training and racing. Had I had access to these principles early on in my career, especially with Coach Stutz's creative presentation, my running would have benefitted greatly, especially as I was learning.

Doug Padilla

From 1981 to 1992 Doug Padilla competed internationally in track and field. A member of the USA National Track and Field Team during that time, he is a veteran of five World Championships and two Olympic Games. He set seven American Records at distances from 3000 meters to 5000 meters, two of which are still current (Indoor 2 Mile and Indoor 5000m). He is the 1985 IAAF Grand Prix Champion, the 1985 IAAF World Cup 5000m Champion, and the 1990 USA Mobil Grand Prix Champion.

Acknowledgements

Is there really such a thing as an original idea? Who I am and what I know, think, say, and write is a direct consequence of my relationships with others. Every person I have interacted with, every speaker I have listened to, every book I have read has formed me into the person I am today. To them goes the credit for what lies written within these pages.

However, at the risk of omitting some, there are a few individuals whom I'd like to acknowledge specifically for the significant impact they have had on my life and the production of this book:

• My parents, Karen Wakefield and Stephen Douglas Stutz, for raising me in the gospel of Jesus Christ and teaching me by example the importance of setting purposeful goals and striving to achieve them.

• My brother, Jim, for introducing me to running by inviting me to do the 600-yard run when I was in the third grade.

• My other brothers— Ron, Bob, Jon—and sister Christine for instilling within me the spirit of teamwork and competition.

• My 4th-6th grade elementary teacher, Richard Lindbloom, for believing in my ability to excel in school and in sports and for making me work hard to achieve success.

• My American Problems high school teacher, Dave Chavis, for showing me the power of teaching and learning by simulating in class what occurs in real life.

• Brigham Young University (BYU) coaches Clarence Robison and Sherald James, for allowing me to compete for the University athletic teams and for demonstrating how to design individualized training programs that meld with a team workout format.

• BYU women's distance coach, Patrick Shane, for sharing his coaching wisdom and for introducing me to the Ricks College program;

• Ferron Sonderegger for inviting me to be his assistant coach at Ricks College, for demonstrating how to coach with firmness and love, and for thirteen memorable years working together.

• Rick College presidents Joe Christensen, Steven Bennion, and David Bednar, and athletic directors Glenn Dalling, Don Rydalch, and Garth Hall, who served at Ricks College since 1987, for their inspired leadership and support of athletics.

• My wife Keysha, for her love, counsel, patience, and sustaining influence.

• The hundreds of student-athletes who chose to participate in cross-country and track & field for Ricks College from 1987-2001, for the wonderfully fulfilling experiences we shared together, learning and growing in athletics, the gospel, and the understanding of success principles.

• God for being my Father, my Redeemer and my Comforter and for enabling me to become who I am and will be.

In putting this book together, I express appreciation to BYU-Idaho students Buffy Holling, LeAnn Hunt, Brian Brown, Katie Hubbard, Steve Shaha, and Andrea Knight for editing the manuscript; Michael Lewis for the photos; Dylan Todd and Bryan Swain for the cover design; Doug Padilla for writing the *Foreword*; former Ricks College Sports Information Director Bryce Rydalch for writing the *About the Author* page; many of my fellow BYU-Idaho employees who have supported this project; and the dozens of Ricks College alumni athletes who contributed memories of their running experiences.

Throughout the pages of this book I have included several success stories of myself and former Ricks College athletes. The intent is not brag or boast. Indeed, I feel as a missionary by the name of Ammon, who once said, "I know that I am nothing; as to my strength I am weak; therefore I will not boast of myself, but I will boast of my God, for in his strength I can do all things."[1] Rather, the intent of sharing these stories is to show by example how, through application of these principles, you can be empowered to gain greater satisfaction from running.

—Preface—   # *The Challenge: How to Race Your Best Every Time*

Do you know runners who perform well in less important races, but falter in "key" competitions; who run well in practices, but don't often race well; or who approach racing with fear and trepidation because of previous racing "failures"? How about runners whose performances fall short of their talent and training, or who run "okay," but never great?

On the other hand, do you know runners who consistently perform well, racing their best when it matters most; who confidently and eagerly look forward to racing, having learned from experience; or whose performances consistently exceed that of others with similar talent and training?

What about you? **What if every time you raced you got the most out of your training?** Is that possible? And if so, how?

As a senior at Brighton High School in Salt Lake City, I had qualified to compete in the Utah State High School Outdoor Track & Field Championships. I remember the anxious bus ride with my school's other track team members up I-15 to Weber State College in Ogden, site of the season's final meet. I hadn't started high school running until that year, so this was my first taste of state track competition. My teammate, a junior whom I had never beaten, toed the starting line with me in the 3200-meter race, along with about twenty other hopeful runners. My previous best time was 10:02. As I anticipated the race, my goal was not to win—I knew there were several more talented runners in the field—but to medal, to finish in the top six. I figured I had to go sub-10:00 (average just under 75 seconds per lap) to do that. I went out the first lap in 73 seconds. Every lap thereafter was a 73, 74, or 75. With a lap to go I found myself well behind the leaders but just behind the 5th place runner and just ahead of my team-mate. I worked hard to gain ground on the runner just ahead, and I could hear my teammate giving it all he had to catch me. I caught and passed the runner in front of me with about 70 meters to go, but couldn't hold off my teammate who out-kicked me to the tape. He didn't want me to think I was better than him, and this deter-mination inspired him to beat me. I was happy to finish 6th in a personal best time of 9:52.

The following day was the 1600-meter final. My teammate and I were once again competing together with twenty of the best high school milers in the state. This race, my focus was totally different. I dreamed of winning. I was going to go out with the leaders and do my best to stay with them. Now my talent in the 1600m was no better than in the 3200m; my PR (personal record) of 4:33 (an average of 68.3 seconds per lap) was probably the 8th or 9th fastest time of the field. I went to the lead quickly and sailed through the first lap in 62 seconds (my PR for the 400-meter dash was only 60 seconds). I was leading the field by a good 10 meters, yet none of the more experienced runners was a bit concerned about me. After another 100 meters, I started to feel the effects of my hasty start. I gradually slowed to catch my breath and to prevent the lactic acid from building up too much in my legs. By the end of the 2nd lap, I found myself in the middle of the pack and losing ground all too swiftly. The third lap I started to fade even more and realized I had been foolish to go out so fast. With one lap to go I was at the back of the strung out pack—in last place. I picked up the pace a bit and caught a handful of runners, but the end result was far below my expectations. I felt embarrassed about my fast start faux pas and later reflected that the state meet was not the place to try to do something that was totally foreign to my previous racing tactics.

Having competed as a distance runner in college and coached for several years since, I have observed runners who are inferior to their peers in training, but consistently out-perform these peers when it matters the most—in key races. I have also observed talented runners who run well race after race. What is it about these runners that enables them to experience consistent success? In what ways do they focus their mental energy to get the most from their physical energy? As a young coach, I concluded if I could figure out what consistently successful runners focused their thoughts on as they prepared for and ran races and teach this in a way that my runners could learn and apply it, then as individuals, as teams, and as a program we would realize greater success and be happier with the results.

As I gathered principles and decided on key words which would aid athletes in remembering them, I discovered that most of the key words began with the letter **P**. So, with a little thought and creativity, I came up with a whole bunch of P-words, even a plethora of them. This book contains many of these principles. As testimony of their effectiveness, I have included several of these runners' stories recounting how applying these P's made a difference in their racing and in their lives. As you apply these P's to your running, you will become a smarter, stronger, faster, and more consistent runner. You will become empowered to race your best!

—Introduction— **Define Success**

How do you define success in racing? Why is success important to you?

One of the keys to successful racing is to first define what success is to you.

Some individuals equate success with winning and anything less than first place with failure. If this equation were true, then few would ever taste success and even fewer would taste it repeatedly. If you considered yourself a loser every time you didn't finish first, your motivation to continue racing would eventually evaporate.

But what if you win a race; does that make you successful? What if the competition is noticeably below your own ability level? If you slack-off in your performance or give less than an honest effort and still win, are you really a success? Perhaps, but you would be hard-pressed to convince yourself and others that you are as successful as the person who gives his all in pursuit of victory. So, to feel consistently rewarded for your running efforts, you are better off not equating success with victory.

SUCCESS ≠ VICTORY

What about equating success with improvement? Regardless of whether you win or lose, as long as you show improvement from one race to the next you can consider yourself a success. However, one drawback with this success formula is that the more you improve, the harder it becomes to continue to improve. Another potential weakness with this formula is in defining what constitutes improvement. Is it running a faster time or finishing in a better place? With the variables of course measurement, terrain, altitude, weather, number of competitors, talent of competitors, etc., a time or place finish difference may or may not mean that you ran any better or worse. So while equating improvement with success may prove valid occasionally, it will not do so consistently. So, for an enduring peace of mind, you shouldn't equate success with improvement.

SUCCESS ≠ IMPROVEMENT

What about defining success as doing your best? This approach certainly appeals to most people. As long as you do your best you are successful, regardless of how fast you run or where you finish. Is this a valid success formula? Certainly. In doing your best can you maximize your success every time you race? Certainly.

However, many runners do not define beforehand what doing their best is. They go into a race saying they will do their best, but then succumb too easily to the pain or the challenges that arise in the heat of the race and finish below their potential. After the race, they rationalize their performance by telling themselves, "Well, I did my best," when they really could have done better if they had made a plan to address the challenges and been better prepared going into the race. So,

SUCCESS ≠ DOING YOUR BEST when you don't clearly define what your best is.

Read that last equation and the preceding paragraph carefully. Doing your best **is** an important **factor** in the equation for lasting success. However, you must also clearly define your best beforehand along with what you can do to attain that level. You must decide how you will meet possible racing challenges, and then you must follow through with your plan. The Cub Scout and Boy Scout mottos combine to accurately describe what it takes to be successful: *Do Your Best* and *Be Prepared*. So,

SUCCESS = DOING YOUR BEST when you clearly define what your best is and act accordingly.

Each chapter of this book teaches you what to think, feel, and do to better prepare for and deal with racing's challenges. By applying these principles you will race smarter, getting the most from the training you have done. You will be able to savor the sweet taste of satisfaction following every race **knowing** you did your best.

Write down your definition for success in running.

Success can be so hard to gauge. During my years of running high school track, I desperately wanted to win an individual state championship. Several times I came agonizingly close—my sophomore year I lost the two-mile by 0.6 seconds. By my senior year winning became my only focus. Although my times improved, I put so much pressure on myself that I wasn't enjoying it anymore. After a disappointing race at state my senior year, I swore off running forever. I soon realized that I was the only one who thought less of myself because of my perceived failure. My not winning a state championship had no effect whatsoever on  how my friends and family felt about me. Now I consider myself successful because I'm still out running, enjoying it, and setting new goals for myself while many of my former competitors have long since quit and moved on to other things.

Ty Draney, Ricks College cross-country and track & field, 1992-1993, 1996. Personal bests: 5000 meters (15:32.1), 100 miles (19:18:25)

Note: Stories by former Ricks College athletes are included at the end of each chapter. The stories are written in the athletes' own words.

Part I:

Pre-Race P's

—Chapter 1—   *Purpose*

Why do you run?

A strong, well-defined purpose empowers you to succeed. It strengthens your resolve and commitment, energizes you to get through difficult obstacles, and focuses your efforts to proceed along your chosen path.

At one of our team meetings at the beginning of the season, I invited our college president, David Bednar, to speak to our athletes. In response to an athlete's question about the purpose of the cross-country program at Ricks College, he observed, "There is really only one reason why we have athletics at Ricks College and that is so others may see the Light of Christ in your countenances."[1] Most people would agree that having such a mission statement for an intercollegiate athletic program is quite unusual. But at Ricks College, it fit perfectly with the college's own mission statement and became a great motivating force behind what we did. President Bednar also promised our athletes that as they diligently strove to realize that purpose, the Lord would strengthen them to perform beyond their natural abilities. Understanding this purpose and exercising faith to receive the promised blessings, our teams and athletes were empowered to win ten national championships—seven women's and three men's—in seven years.

Clearly understanding your purpose for running and believing in the benefits that will accrue as you pursue that purpose will focus your thoughts and actions to achieve your goals.

In the Book of Mormon, Captain Moroni led the Nephite armies many times against the invading Lamanites who intended *"to destroy [them] or to subject them and bring them into bondage that they might establish a kingdom unto themselves over all the land.*"[2] Contrast this purpose with that of the Nephites:

Nevertheless, the Nephites were inspired by a better cause, for they were not fighting for monarchy nor power but they were fighting for their homes and their liberties, their wives and their children, and their all, yea, for their rites of worship and their church.[3]

In one particular battle, as the tide turned in favor of the Lamanite armies, the Nephites' courage faltered:

And it came to pass that when the men of Moroni saw the fierceness and the anger of the Lamanites, they were about to shrink and flee from them.[4]

Nevertheless, a reminder of their purpose turned the tide again:

And Moroni, perceiving their intent, sent forth and inspired their hearts with these thoughts—yea, the thoughts of their lands, their liberty, yea, their freedom from bondage. And it came to pass that they turned upon the Lamanites, and they cried with one voice unto the Lord their God, for their liberty and their freedom from bondage. And they began to stand against the Lamanites with power; and in that selfsame hour that they cried unto the Lord for their freedom, the Lamanites began to flee before them.[5]

Notice that when his men were about to give up, Moroni reminded them of their **purpose** for fighting. Remembering their purpose, they turned from fleeing and toward fighting the enemy with renewed determination. They unitedly cried unto the Lord with faith that He would strengthen them to achieve their goal— victory in battle—in order to realize their purpose. Soon after they acted, the Nephites were strengthened by the Lord in a powerful manner to stand against the Lamanites and cause them to flee.

Following the victorious battle *"the people of Nephi were exceedingly rejoiced, because the Lord had again delivered them out of the hands of their enemies; therefore they gave thanks unto the Lord their God; yea, and they did fast much and pray much, and they did worship God with exceedingly great joy."*[6]

Like the Nephites, you too will be strengthened to accomplish your goals in powerful ways when you focus on your purpose before, during, and after you race. With a clear understanding of your running purpose, you will be willing to do the work necessary to prepare to race well. Recalling that purpose as you race will strengthen your resolve to face head-on challenges as they arise instead of faltering along the way. Remembering your running purpose after you finish will help you keep in perspective the race outcome.

To really excel in anything you must be driven by a purpose. If you aren't sure why you race, you will eventually quit when obstacles arise...not **if** the obstacles arise but **when**. They always come.

Obstacles may come from external sources—family, friends, or associates who do not share or understand your passion for running. Obstacles may surface from internal sources—aches, injuries, or time constraints that force you to curtail your training. Whatever the obstacles, sooner or later they'll appear insurmountable unless your purpose is more important than giving in. If you are passionate about your purpose, you will stay committed long past the time when others have abandoned their running shoes.

So, what is your purpose for running? You probably have several purposes for running, although one likely stands out as most important. Following is a list of some of the more common running purposes. As you contemplate these and other purposes, consider these questions:

Does this purpose accurately describe why you run?

Do some purposes movitate you more powerfully than others?

1. Get or stay physically fit
2. Lose or maintain weight
3. Magnify existing talent
4. Feel more alert physically, mentally, and spiritually
5. Make or cultivate friendships
6. Belong to a group of people who share a common interest

7. Attract attention of those of the opposite gender
8. Be recognized for good performance
9. Be popular
10. Prove something to somebody
11. Be better than others in something
12. Honor or please others
13. Strengthen self-confidence
14. Develop good work habits
15. Develop leadership abilities
16. Use running achievement to develop credibility to persuade others more effectively
17. Have fun
18. Win money or scholarship
19. Win awards

In addition to having a purpose for running, you should also establish a purpose for each race. With a clear understanding of why you are running a race, you can wisely focus your effort. You will view each race as a stepping stone and not as an end in itself. You will know that, win or lose, you will learn something from the race that will help you in the future.

Possible purposes for a race include the following:

1. Discover or measure current state of fitness and racing ability
2. Develop or test a particular racing strategy
3. Gain experience racing under conditions similar to those anticipated in a future key race
4. Make a significant contribution to the team's or another runner's success

As you ponder your purpose for a specific race, keep in mind that it should motivate you to succeed in that specific race *and* in your overarching running purpose.

Write down your purposes for running. Identify which purpose is most important to you.

Write down your purpose for your next race.

I learned a valuable lesson about running during my final cross-country season at Ricks College: there is a joy that far surpasses any and all pleasure associated with times, places and bragging rights.

In a meeting prior to the commencement of the 1999 cross-country season, we met at Coach's house and set a goal of finishing among the top three teams at the national final. We listed what time each individual would need run in order to meet that goal. Some of that meeting was dedicated to identifying

specific individual sacrifices we would each make: proper rest, nutrition, training, and balanced social and academic life, to name a few. One point stood out: **"Represent yourself, your family, your school, and your religion in a manner that cultivates not only a spirit of excellence but one of genuine kindness and charity for others wherever and whenever you travel."** This became our goal, pushing the national placings to a secondary concern. Promises were exchanged and we began our season.

In a later meeting, Ricks College President David A. Bednar promised us that if we accomplished our goal of being the best example we could be, on and off the field, we would not only reach our secondary goals, but we would far exceed what we originally thought possible.

The fulfillment of his promise was nothing less than spectacular: a new NJCAA championship meet record for an all-time low team score. Seven runners among the top twenty-one finishers. A 21-second spread between our fifth and first man. And a national title.

All of these accomplishments continue to rank a **very** distant second when placed next to the friendships I made that season. Those guys became my brothers. At one point in the national race when I contemplated giving in, thinking I'd gone out too fast, the thought of disappointing any of those men pushed me through the pain and on to a 50-second personal best. I have since run personal bests at numerous other distances, but my fastest 8K is still that race.

If all you get out of running is times and places, **you are missing out**. Your excellence on the track should flood into every corner of your life off the track. There is nothing like being part of a group of good people pushing each other onwards and upwards to higher levels of excellence. There is no limit to the happiness. No salary cap. No well that may run dry. This aspect of running has made my life **full.** I will be forever grateful to Coach, Ricks College (now BYU-Idaho), and my teammates for the priceless gift of this knowledge.

Michael Thatcher, Ricks College cross-country and track & field teams, 1995-1996, 1999-2000. Led Vikings to 1999 National Junior College Athletic Association (NJCAA) cross-country title in Lansing, Michigan, finishing the 8,000 meter course in seventh place in 25:07.

—Chapter 2— *Purposeful Goals*

Goals are different from purposes, although the two terms are often used interchangeably. Purpose is the **why** behind what you do. Goals are **what** you strive to do to fulfill your purpose. With an understanding of why you run, set meaningful, productive goals.

When writing your goals, express them as if you were already doing them or had already accomplished them. Writing them in this way programs the mind to believe and expect the goals to be achieved and sets in motion the processes to bring them to fruition.[1]

For example, if your purpose for running is to get or stay physically fit, possible season goals could include the following:
1. I am running 60 minutes/day, 5 days a week
2. I am lifting weights and doing flexibility and strength training exercises twice a week
3. I eat three nutritious meals a day
4. I sleep 7-8 hours each night

If you do not have a running purpose other than to get or stay physically fit, then you will probably not be motivated to race. You will remain content to just train as that will be sufficient to realize your purpose.

However, if your purpose for running includes to magnify your existing talent and to be better than others, then possible season goals could include the following:
1. I have run 15:37 for 5000 meters (or some other time faster than your current abilities)
2. I have placed in the top 10 at the Region Championships (or some other place better than your previous placing)

With that purpose for running, a possible purpose for a race might be to develop or test your ability to use a particular racing strategy, such as running an even-paced race. If your goal time is 15:37 for a 5000-meter race on the track (12½ laps on a 400-meter track), your even-paced race goal would be to run each 400-meter lap in 75 seconds. Can you envision how you can set productive goals based on your pre-determined purpose?

Based on you purposes for running, write down goals for the season or year.

Based on your purpose, write down goals for your next race.

When I started collegiate athletics, I wasn't particularly gifted. Like every other high school runner, I had run 2 minutes in the 800-meters, and 50 seconds in the 400-meters. However, I had two of the most important characteristics: a dream and the persistence to accomplish it.

I clearly remember my first few weeks of cross-country practice; my brother and I arrived at school after averaging no more than 30 miles a week over the summer. Our first day of practice, we went for a ten-mile run. Being new in town, I didn't know the roads or even how to get back to the school. After the first couple of miles our teammates weren't even in sight. My brother and I were so far behind that when we finally made it back to the locker room, most of the guys had finished showering and were heading home for the day.

At that moment my brother and I made the decision that we would not only make the team, but we would someday be top runners. That wasn't the only time I remember finishing alone; in fact, for the first couple of weeks it was a routine occurrence. However, as time went on we gradually found ourselves a little closer to the other runners at the end of workouts until eventually we were running every workout with the team. We made our goals small at first; we just wanted to be able to run an entire workout with the team. Then over time our goals evolved to include much grander accomplishments, such as attaining All-American honors and winning a national team title.

After all the grueling work, our persistence finally paid off. Only a few months after arriving at Ricks College, I placed third on the team at the National meet, our team won the NJCAA National Championship, and I received Honorable Mention All-American honors. If there is one thing I learned from this experience it is that if you set your mind to something and are persistent, even in the face of insurmountable odds, eventually you will see all of your dreams become reality.

Dustin Trail, Ricks College cross-country and track & field, 1999-2000. Personal best 1500-meter time of 3:45.19.

—Chapter 3—   *Plan*

Develop a strategy to accomplish your purpose. Plan what to do to achieve your purpose before taking action. Evaluate options and make decisions based on what you feel is the best course of action to follow.

As the Ricks College cross-country coach, I was constantly thinking about what to do to prepare our athletes to be successful in the future. I concur with the counsel of noted author and speaker Stephen R. Covey to **Begin with the End in Mind.**[1]

When writing workouts for the season, I began by picturing the condition of the athletes in mid-June, then envisioning the condition they could be in by the championship meet in mid-November. I knew what our purpose was for running cross-country and kept that at the forefront in the planning process. I scheduled our season's meets according to which would best prepare us to accomplish that purpose.

Next, I planned the season's workouts, one week at a time, using a combination of components to develop, change, and improve the athletes in gradual and specific ways. I continued until I had the entire season of workouts organized on an 8.5" x 11" sheet of paper, complete with training site, type, frequency, duration, pace, rest, warm-up and cool-down periods, and weekly training volume. (See a sample season workout sheet on page 30.) This master workout plan was subject to change based on the athletes' feedback and how they responded to the training. Although the master workout plan was usually followed quite closely, a season didn't go by where some modifications to the plan weren't made to adjust to the athletes' responses. Every year as I looked forward to working with the incoming and returning runners, I would rewrite the workouts to address those things I had learned the previous year.

As you develop a plan to achieve your running purpose, be sure to do the following:
1. Start from where you are.
2. Learn from past history.
3. Focus on desired outcomes.
4. Be reasonably optimistic.
5. Focus on key races.
6. Plan for gradual and specific improvement.
7. Have a simple, specific plan.
8. Be able to adapt.

Long-term Planning

1. Start from where you are.

If you are currently running 3 miles per day, 3 times per week, for 28-30 minutes, and you have been doing so for only 3 weeks, you would not be wise to pick up the latest magazine listing an elite marathoner's training schedule and think you could suddenly jump your training to that level. Doing so would most likely lead to injury or discouragement. A more practical approach would be to consult a coach or book that could help you design a training program geared toward your specific talent, allotted training time, and desires. If you would like my recommendation of what coach or book to consult, refer to "Recommended Books" on page 133 or contact me at the address given on the last page.

2. Learn from past history.

If you have done things in the past that have brought about positive results, you probably ought to include them in your current and future plans. Likewise, if some your training choices have led to injury or other negative results, you ought to rethink the value of repeating them. However, keep in mind that benefits derived from some training do not manifest themselves immediately. Some benefits are recognizable only after several weeks— sometimes even months—of training. So don't discontinue a planned training program until you have given it ample time to bear fruit. One exception to this is when you feel an injury coming on that would worsen if you continued the course of training.

3. Focus on desired outcomes.

Visualize where you want to be and what you want to achieve at the end of your goal time frame. Everything you do should be done with these questions in mind: Will doing this help me to realize my goal and purpose? If so, how? Will doing this put my goals at risk? If so, what could I do to minimize or eliminate the risk?

4. Be reasonably optimistic.

Expect yourself to develop, change, and improve as you follow your training program. Expect yourself to become faster, stronger, and more efficient. Expect that you will remain healthy and injury-free. Exert faith in your training partners, coach, and others involved—they are strong assets. Expect to train well. Expect to race well. Expect to learn something valuable from each practice and race. Plan, believing you will realize your purpose and achieve your goals. Sincerely believe you can achieve these goals; they must be more than mere wishes or fantasies.

5. Focus on key races.

In most communities these days, there is a plethora of races to run in any given week of the running season. Some individuals, who may not understand your vision and mission, may urge you to compete in more events than are in your best interest. If you have control over your race schedule, plan to compete only in those events that will best prepare you to achieve your goals and purposes. If, as part of a team, you are forced to race more often than you would like, view these extra races more as workouts or opportunities to help a slower teammate run a little faster.

6. Plan for gradual and specific improvement.

Plan your workouts so that you increase the volume, intensity, or density of specific training gradually over time. A good rule of thumb is to increase your volume of a specific type of training no more than 10% per week. As you approach your most important races, it's a good idea to reduce the volume of your training a bit to allow time to rest, recover, and rebuild. The greater the volume of specific training, the greater this rest should be in terms of length and volume.

7. Make a simple, specific plan.

Knowing where you are now and where you want to be at the end of the goal time period, write out your plan to get there. Do not include a lot of detail. Keep your plan simple so you can understand and conceptualize in your mind what you are going to do and how you are going to do it. As you gain experience in making and executing a plan, you can add additional details.

8. Be adaptable.

Running, like life, is very dynamic by nature. In spite of your best-laid plans, things occur during running seasons that force you to alter your plans.

For example, you may have to deal with injuries or the pain of pre-injuries. What do you do when this happens? Do you keep training through the injury and hope it goes away? Do you stop training altogether until the injury is completely healed? You should probably counsel with a coach, athletic trainer, or sport physician for some possible ideas.

With some creative thinking, you can almost always find a way to adapt and keep going. David Bednar, while serving as president of BYU-Idaho, was asked by a student-athlete, "What is the most important lesson to learn while competing in athletics?" His response was, "To not quit when you feel like quitting."[2] If you are diligent, you can almost always find a way to continue on when times get tough.

Race Planning

As you anticipate competing, follow the same steps to devise a race plan as you did when developing a training plan.

1. Start from where you are.

Let's say you ran a 5-kilometer race two weeks ago in a PR (personal record) time of 22:00—about 7 minute/mile pace—and now you're lining up to race against several runners whose PRs are around 17:30. It would probably not be wise to run the first part of the race with the leaders. Doing so would likely exhaust you early in the race, forcing you to slow down drastically as the event progressed. A better plan would be to start the race at a pace close to 7 minute/mile pace, maintain that pace throughout the race, and finish with a kick (faster pace) over the last quarter-mile. Don't force yourself to run at someone else's pace; start from where you are.

2. Learn from past history.

As you make a race plan for yourself, start by following a plan similar to the one you used to achieve recent success. There are times when you will want to experiment using different race strategies to see how they affect your racing. However, because of the risk involved in implementing an unfamiliar strategy, you should stick to a familiar race plan for your most important races.

3. Focus on desired outcomes.

Visualize what place you will finish in, what time the clock will read, and how you will feel as you cross the finish line. Then picture yourself running the race confidently from beginning to end.

4. Be reasonably optimistic.

Always toe the starting line believing you will have a successful race. If an experienced coach feels you are ready to race faster than previously, then go ahead and consider starting out faster.

Otherwise, plan to start the race at a pace right at or just slightly faster than what your training would indicate. Even if you aren't feeling in prime physical condition, plan to run successfully anyway. I have witnessed many runners run good, even great races, when they were feeling less than 100% healthy or injury-free.

5. Focus on key races.

Often I see near-sighted coaches and athletes who treat every race as if it were the most important race of the season. If a race is worth racing, it's worth resting for. Racing too frequently can dampen your mental and physical freshness and, consequently, lessen racing success as the season progresses. Choose carefully those races you will enter. Consider how each will help or hamper your long-term goals and purposes.

6. Plan for gradual and specific improvement.

Race as you have trained and prepared yourself. For example, if you have never trained or raced in racing spikes before, a race is not a good time to try them out. Your muscles will be much better prepared and you will feel more confident racing in spikes when you have done some hard training (similar to racing) in them beforehand. Likewise, you will race stronger over a hilly course when you have included some race-pace uphill and downhill running in your training.

7. Make a simple, specific plan.

Lining up at the starting line without a clue about the course or the competition can be a recipe for disappointment. Going over the course beforehand so you know what to expect from the terrain and layout can provide you invaluable information for planning your race strategy.

For example, if there are steep hills at both the beginning and ending stages of the course, you will probably want to keep your pace in check on the first set of hills, avoiding premature lactic acid build-up. Having studied the course, you will recognize when you reach the final stages of the race and feel confident attacking the hills there.

Knowing the course beforehand gives you an idea of where you are in relation to the total distance of the race. You can plan with confidence the pace you want to run and the position you want to be in at various stages of the race. Armed with this knowledge, you can plan where to give yourself cues to maintain or pick up your pace, stay with or pass competitors, or kick it in to the finish. Racing with a plan, you can constantly evaluate how you are doing and make adjustments to get yourself back on target if you deviate even slightly.

8. Be adaptable.

Most of the time, in spite of all your careful planning, something unexpected in the course, the competition, or the weather will arise. I remember running in a big race in Pasco, Washington, where the lead pack of 12 runners were told to run the wrong way at a fork near the 1.5-mile mark of a 5-mile race. The error was soon noticed by the race officials, who directed the remaining runners to follow the correct route. In the meantime other race officials labored to get the lead pack back on the right course without having them stop, turn around, and retrace their steps to where they were led off course. When this lead pack was finally guided back to the right course, they found themselves near the 3-mile mark about 150 meters behind the current leader and with about 20 other runners in front of them. How would you respond if you were one of these 12 runners who had been led off course? A few of them shouted and complained to let everyone around them know that they had been wronged. One dropped out. But a few took off in hot pursuit, determined to do their best to work their way back toward the front. Two of them were Ricks College athletes, Ryan Jenks and David Woodbury. Ryan and David finished 7th and 12th, respectively. Had they not taken the wrong turn, Ryan probably would have finished in the top three and David in the top six. However, upon finishing, they each knew they had raced probably their best ever. Each could claim, *"I have fought the good fight, I have finished the course, I have kept the faith."*[3] And their teammates were further convinced that *"they were exceedingly valiant for courage; and also for strength and activity; [and] they were men who were true at all times in whatsoever thing they were entrusted."*[4] So when unforeseen obstacles arise—as they often do—stay cool, don't complain, and do your best to succeed in spite of them. Your ability to adapt to change is often the catalyst that propels you to a higher level of achievement.

If you approach racing with a "whatever" attitude—failing to plan—you will reap "whatever" results. Taking time to prepare— to make a plan for what you desire to do and to accomplish—will greatly increase your ability to realize your desires.

Write down a long-term plan to achieve your running purposes and goals.

Write down a plan to prepare for your next race.

Write down a strategic plan for your next race.

Caution: The workout schedule on the following page is provided as an example of a simple, specific training plan. I gave such a plan to each of our athletes as they arrived on campus in the fall to train as a team. It's founded on the premise that each of the athletes followed a similar pre-season training plan on their own during the summer. It was written for a specific set of athletes with specific goals and specific "prices" they were willing to pay (see "Price" on page 33). Explaining all that goes into developing a workout schedule is beyond the scope and intent of this book. For a list of books that do treat this subject, refer to "Recommended Books" on page 133. **This workout schedule is not intended nor should it be construed as a recommended plan for you to follow. Indeed, following a training plan designed specifically for someone else may be detrimental to your performance and health.**

Cross-Country Fall Workout Schedule—Men[5]

		Monday	Tuesday	Wednesday	Thursday	Friday	Saturday	Miles
Aug 27- Sep 01	AM	0-45' easy run	45' easy run ST +10 & 10	45'@E hills +10 & 10 green canyon 0-45' easy bike/run	45' easy bike/run ST +10 & 10	45' easy run w/ 2x1' strides	4 mile time trial golf course	57/75
	PM	4x6'@T w/1' +15 & 10 intramural field	technique +10 & 10		technique +10 & 10	0-45' easy bike/run		
Sep 3-8	AM	85-100' easy run w/6x30" strides	ST +10 & 10	0-45' easy run	ST +10 & 10	0-45' easy run	90-105' easy run	65/83
	PM	golf course	40' easy run w/ technique	6x1200m@T w/45" +10 & 10 intramural field	45' easy run/bike w/technique	24 stadium stairs +15 & 15		
Sep 10-15	AM	0-45' easy run	ST +10 & 10	0-45' easy run	ST +10 & 10	0-45' easy run	MSU Invite in Bozeman, MT	55/73
	PM	6-7x800m hills@I w/jog recovery +15 & 10 water tower	40' easy run w/ technique	60'@E +10 & 10 farm road	45' easy run/bike w/technique	45' easy run w/ 2x400m@R	8k race	
Sep 17-22	AM	0-45' easy run	ST +10 & 10	0-45' easy run: Stepping Stone: 8krp+2.25'↓15" p5' +15 & 10 green canyon	ST +10 & 10	0-45' easy run	100-110' easy run	63/84
	PM	70-80' easy run/bike	40' easy run w/ technique		45' easy run/bike	12x400m@R w/2.75' +15 & 10 technique track		
Sep 24-29	AM	0-45' easy run	ST +10 & 10	0-45' easy run	ST +10 & 10	0-45' easy run	Big Cross Meet in Pasco, WA	53/72
	PM	5-6x1000m hills@I w/jog recovery +15 & 10 arboretum	3x20' games of ultimate football +10 & 10 soccer field	60'@E +10 & 10 sugar city cemetery	45' easy run/bike w/6x30" strides	40' easy run w/ 2x400m@R	8k race	
Oct 1-06	AM	ST +10 & 10	0-45' easy run	0-45' easy run	ST +10 & 10	0-45' easy run	90-100' easy run	63/85
	PM	70-80' easy run golf course	5x1600m@I w/ 3.5' +15 & 15 golf course	50' easy run/bike	50' easy run w/ technique	21'@T w/5' 4x400m@R w/ 2.75' +15 & 15 golf course	hilly	
Oct 8-13	AM	0-45' easy run	ST +10 & 10	0-45' easy run	0-45' easy run	0-20' easy run	70-80' easy run w/6x30" strides	48/81
	PM	Stepping Stone: 8krp+1.75'↓15" p5' +15 & 15 golf course	50' easy run/bike	70-80' easy run w/ technique golf course	40' easy run w/ 2x400m@R golf course	Utah State Invite in Logan, UT 8k race		
Oct 15-20	AM	0-45' easy run	ST +10 & 10	0-45' easy run	ST +10 & 10	0-45' easy run	95-110' easy run	59/79
	PM	7x1200m@T w/45" +15 & 15 golf course	50' easy run	24 stadium stairs +15 & 15	50' easy run w/ 6x30" strides	50' easy run w/ technique golf course	hilly	
Oct 22-27	AM	0-45' easy run	ST +10 & 10	0-35' easy run	ST +10 & 10		Region 18 Meet at Municipal Golf Course	54/65
	PM	21'@T w/5' 4x400m@R w/2.75' +15 & 15 golf course	50' easy run	4x1200m@T w/45"/3' 2x800m@I w/1'/4' 2x200m@R w/90" +15 & 15 golf course	40' easy run w/ 6x30" strides	40' easy run w/ 2x400m@R golf course	8k race	
Oct 29- Nov 03	AM	ST +10 & 10	0-35' easy run	ST +10 & 10	0-35' easy run		50-60' easy run w/4x30" strides	54/68
	PM	70-80' easy run	4x800m@T w/30"/3' 4x800m@I w/1'/4' 4x400m@R w/2.75' +15 & 15 golf course	40' easy run w/ 4x30" strides	3x1600m@Tw/1'/4' 2x800m@I w/1'/4' 2x200m@R w/90" +15 & 15 golf course	40' easy run		
Nov 5-10	AM	0-30' easy run	ST +10 & 10	0-30' easy run	Fly to Detroit	30-40' easy run w/ 2x400m@R	NJCAA Championships in Lansing, MI	42/50
	PM	2400m@T w/5' 1600m@I-5" +15 & 15 golf course	40' easy run	3x1200m@T w/45"/3' 2x400m@R w/2.75' +15 & 15 golf course	35' easy run w/ 3x400m@R	on course	8k race	

As athletes at Ricks College, one of the first things we did each season was to sit down as a team and individually, to establish specific goals. The goals we set were not general accomplishments we hoped to achieve during the season, but a specific and realistic map, taking into consideration past years' performances and all of the variables that would go into helping us achieve our new goals. Because we developed a detailed strategy, I felt there was no question whether or not we'd achieve our purpose. All that was left to do was execute the plan.

Brick Bergeson, Ricks College cross-country and track & field, 1995-1996, 1998-1999. Personal bests: 1500 meters (3:42.7); 800 meters (1:48.39)

—Chapter 4—   *Price*

Almost invariably as you move forward with your training, unanticipated costs arise. If it's your first time training as a distance runner and you haven't done a great deal of study or research in running, these unanticipated costs may be significant and appear frequently. If you are a seasoned runner, the unexpected costs likely arise less frequently and may be more easily dealt with. Knowing that unanticipated costs will arise should not keep you from starting to run in the first place. "Take a step into the darkness, exercising faith that the light will follow."[1] The closer you get to realizing your goal, the more determined you'll be to complete it, and the less likely it is that unanticipated costs will sway your decision to proceed.

Understanding what's involved in achieving success and making sure you are willing, able, and committed to do what is necessary to achieve success are fundamental before starting any worthwhile endeavor.

For which of you, intending to build a tower, sitteth not down first, and counteth the cost, *whether he have sufficient to finish it? Lest haply, after he hath laid the foundation, and is not able to finish it, all that behold it begin to mock him, Saying, This man began to build, and was not able to finish.*[2]

At the beginning of every season at Ricks College, we gathered as a cross-country team to discuss our team vision and goals. Together we reviewed what our teams had achieved in the past, the anticipated strength of our competitors, and what level of team performance would be required by the end of the season to attain certain levels of accomplishment. I concluded the presentation by expressing what I believed they could accomplish as a team. My vision was always high yet realistic. It was not some pie-in-the-sky wish, but something that I actually believed could be done if the team and I did everything we could to bring it to fruition. I then let the team members discuss and decide among themselves what the team vision and goals would be. Almost every year, the team's vision and goals would match those I had shared with them. On a couple of occasions, the team set goals that were even higher.

Once the team vision and goals were set, I would meet one-by-one with each team member to discuss his or her role in achieving the team goals, and his or her individual goals. We would also discuss what he or she would commit to do to realize those goals—that is, the price he or she was willing to pay.

The law of the harvest states, "You reap what you sow." So it is with running and every other worthwhile pursuit: a high altitude goal requires a high altitude price.

Here are areas in which you should determine the price you will pay and commit to it:
1. Time
2. Discomfort/Pain
3. Commitment/Long-term Dedication
4. Good Nutrition
5. Sleep
6. Gain knowledge of running
7. Social activities
8. Personal desires for the good of a team

1. Time

Training your body to be a successful distance runner requires time to dress, warm up, work out, cool down, stretch, shower, and dress again every time you exercise. How much time will you set aside for this each day, and how many days of the week will you train? For example, say your goal-based workout plan calls for you to run 40 miles per week. While training, if on average you run a mile in 9 minutes, you would need to run 360 minutes for the week. If you run 6 days/week, you would need to average 60 minutes per day. In addition you would need to allow time for dressing, warming up and cooling-down, etc. If you figure 30 minutes for these other activities, you would need to commit 90 minutes/day, 6 days/week in order to follow your workout plan. If you didn't have this much time available, you would have to either create more time to train or reduce your planned training volume and, consequently, your goals and expectations.

2. Discomfort/Pain

There are two types of pain you can experience as a direct result of running: injury-related pain, normally caused by over-or misuse, and fatigue pain, caused by the build up of lactic acid in the muscles.

In terms of the injury-related pain, the price you need to consider is how much effort you will put into preventing it by buying proper shoes, doing strength-training, choosing training volume and locations carefully, and stretching; treating it by icing, taping, cross-training, massage and/or other treatments; and dealing with it by training and racing through the injury. The less critical a race is to your long-term running goals, the less willing you should be to risk further injury by racing.

Pain induced by fatiguing muscles, though not a desireable sensation, is not something you should readily give in to when it comes. Often the difference in performance between two runners of equal talent and ability is that the winner is willing to push through the pain. Making the decision that you are willing to pay that price when it is required can be a key to your success. (For ideas on how to deal with fatigue pain when it occurs, see *"Persist through the Pain " on page 95*.)

3. Commitment/Long-term Dedication

Being a successful distance runner requires a long-term perspective. You should realize improvement will come one step at a time, one crunch at a time, one focused thought at a time, one healthy meal at a time, and one minute of sleep at a time, repeated hundreds, and thousands, and even millions of times over the course of days, weeks, months, and years. And yet the improvement you realize because of that one more step, crunch, thought, banana, or other training component will not be recognizable at the moment you do it nor may it be for several days or weeks in the future. In fact—and this is prevalent when beginning a new training program—you may feel even worse than you did before you started. In this world of instant gratification and instant results, you may feel tempted to quit or reduce your vision or goals before you have even begun, let alone finished. That is why paying the price of making a long-term commitment and being dedicated enough to honor that commitment on a consistent basis is vital to achieving success. (For more detail on making and keeping commitments, see *"Pact " on page 45*.)

4. Good Nutrition

I've often heard this analogy: the human body is like a well-engineered automobile. If you fuel each properly, it runs great, but if you put junk in for fuel it will run poorly and eventually break down.

In the case of the automobile, that breakdown can be drastic and immediate. I know. Once while traveling across the country, my car started sputtering, misfiring and chugging its way down the highway. Unable to continue safely on the road, I exited and found a service station. When I explained to the attendant this sudden and drastic change in my vehicle's performance, he said, "It's because you bought some gasoline with water in it." One tank of bad fuel was enough to destroy my car's performance. In this sense, the human body is not like a well-engineered automobile. Usually one bad meal is not enough to severely affect your running performance. Unfortunately, some faster runners seem to eat just about anything—be it chocolate mousse, cola, or greasy hamburgers—or in some cases, just about nothing—a few leaves of lettuce for instance—and still run fast the next day. As a result, many athletes do not concern themselves much about their diet.

Although the food you eat does not appear to have the immediate effect upon your body's performance that fuel has on an automobile, it does, in the long run, affect your body's ability to run long. A healthier diet strengthens your body's ability to withstand disease or injury, and it provides a better source of energy for running, studying, working, or doing a multitude of other worthwhile activities. It also creates a fitter home in which your spirit can thrive.

5. Sleep

Getting adequate, consistent rest rejuvenates the body as it recovers from the stress of daily life. High school and college-age students engaged in a full load of classes and participating on athletic teams, should be getting between 7-9 hours per night. Getting to bed and getting up at consistent times every day are also important factors in the rejuvenation process, preferably getting to bed early and getting up early.

In my years of coaching at Ricks College, I can recall only one distance runner who performed well consistently without adhering to these sleep standards. Most people—especially students—undervalue the power that sleep has to enable their bodies to recover, rebuild, and perform at high levels.

If you live or associate closely with people who do not understand this principle, they may mock and belittle you at first for deciding to be different. However, in time they will grow to respect and admire you and perhaps even follow your example as you implement these sleep standards. Don't you be one who scoffs at paying the price of sufficient rest.

6. Gaining knowledge of running

If you are part of a running group or team, you may feel you can rely on the coach or group leader to explain all you need to know to reach your goals. If you are training on your own or if you do not have a confident coach or group leader, you may want to gain at least a basic running knowledge to be successful and avoid injury. Even if your group or team is led by a trusted and seasoned coach, you still benefit from better understanding the principles that lead to running success. The better you understand these principles, the greater your confidence will be that your training plan will accomplish your goals.

The best way to gain this knowledge is through study and by faith. Study by asking questions of successful runners and coaches. Search for and read good books. Try to make sense out of what you learn from these resources. Act with faith in the plan you decide to follow. As you experience success by applying correct principles, you gain greater understanding and wisdom which will empower you to act with even greater faith in the future. Are you content with your knowledge and understanding of correct running principles? What price are you willing to pay to increase it?

7. Social activities

Certainly social activities are an important ingredient to a healthy lifestyle. In fact, one of the prime reasons you may be a runner is because of the social interaction you have with other runners. But some runners, especially some student runners, find they have to curtail some of their social activities in order to put in the time and honor the commitments necessary to be successful runners. If this sounds like your situation, what social activities are you willing—happily willing—to give up? I say "happily willing" because if you are grumpy about having to sacrifice, you will not gain as much from your running as you would if you trained with a good attitude.[3] So what are you happily willing to give up?

8. Personal desires for the good of a team

Whenever you're part of a group, you have to compromise some of your personal wishes for the group to move forward as a team. In running, this may mean you eat Italian food with the team the night before a big race when, if you had had your preference, you would have chosen soup and salad. It may mean you start a race at a pace slightly slower or faster than you would personally choose in order to help your teammates draw on the strength that comes from running together as a team. It may mean when you entertain thoughts of slowing down during a race, you decide instead to dig a little deeper, to persist a little longer because you don't want to let your team down. How much are you willing to sacrifice in terms of personal preferences, wishes, or comforts so you can contribute to a more powerful, unified, and successful team?

Before you commit to pursue a worthwhile running goal, you should count the costs and determine if you are willing to pay the price. If after counting the costs you decide it is more than you wish to pay, rethink your goal, and bring it more in line with a price you are willing to pay. Doing so will save you hours of pain and frustration.

When pursuing a running goal whose price you understand and are committed to pay, you are much more prepared to meet the challenges that arise along the way. You will not continually stop en route to weigh the option of not going running today because it's cold, or because your friends want you to be social, or because you just aren't in the mood at the moment. You will have already made that decision, so you can press forward, undaunted in the quest of achieving your goal.

Write down the commitment and sacrifices are you willing to make to achieve your running purposes.

Write down what you will commit to do to be successful in your next race.

"Prepare" is probably the mantra of my life. My mother raised me to be practical—if I didn't have a plan for the future, I would end up wherever life placed me. Knowing how "fair" life can be, I motivated myself to decide what I wanted and execute the steps required to achieve that position. I wanted to run at Ricks College! I knew that I didn't have the raw talent to make the team, so I would have to rely on my heart and extensive preparation.

I knew that I would have to start early and be consistent. This meant diligently following the summer workout provided. It meant getting up at 6 am to workout because my outdoor summer job would sap my energy by the end of the day. It meant simulating the racing season: going to bed early, eating properly, drinking enough water, stretching, and warming up.

I wasn't the best runner at Ricks, but I ran on the Ricks College team. There were probably lots of people who were better runners than me. My preparation was the key to my success. Success is measured differently for everyone. My success was being on the team, giving 100%, and trying to learn something on the way. I think I did.

Teri Cordova Barrett, Ricks College cross-country and track & field, 1994-1995. Personal best: mile (5:27)

—Chapter 5—   *Pact*

Once you define your purpose, map out a plan, and determine the price you are willing to pay, you are ready to make pacts. Binding yourself to yourself, God, and possibly a coach or person close to you helps solidify your commitment and strengthen your resolve; you invoke their assistance in helping you achieve success. Covenant to pay the price as you embark upon a course of action.

A pact is a binding agreement or commitment. It represents the strongest type of decision you can make. Its strengths come from the fact that it—
1. Solidifies your decision to act
2. Is not easily forgotten
3. Adds an accountability to report your actions
4. Invokes the assistance of the other parties involved

As I mentioned in the chapter on Price, at the beginning of every season at Ricks College, we gathered as a cross-country team to discuss our team vision and goals. Once the team vision and goals were set, I met one-on-one with the team members to discuss their roles in achieving the team's and their individual goals. Each member of the team submitted to me in writing a detailed and specific statement of commitment. Each week during the season, I visited one-on-one with team members, where they accounted for their part of the pact. We discussed how we felt about their progress toward achieving their goals and what adjustments might be made to improve progress.

Meeting each week to discuss their progress instilled in the athletes a greater sense of duty to honor their commitments, and provided me, the coach, with valuable feedback. From the information shared in these meetings, I determined if athletes' training plans needed to be adjusted, if they needed to better live by their commitments, or if the current plan and performance level were already in line with expectations. These regular short visits were vital to keeping us on target throughout the season.

To clarify and better remember your pact, write down specifically what you covenant to do. Make a commitment to yourself and to someone who cares about you (such as your coach, spouse, or close friend) defining what price you will pay to succeed. If you run to give glory to God, be sure to make a pact with Him, too.

When you make pacts, you are strengthened and enabled to do more than you otherwise would. As W.H. Murray expounded:

Until one is committed there is hesitancy, the chance to draw back, always ineffectiveness. Concerning all acts of initiative (and creation), there is one elemental truth, the ignorance of which kills countless ideas and splendid plans: that the moment one definitely commits oneself, then Providence moves, too. All sorts of things occur to help one that would never otherwise have occurred. A whole stream of events issues from the decision, raising in one's favor all manner of unforeseen incidents and meetings and material assistance, which no man could have dreamt would have come his way.[1]

Write down a pact you will use to achieve your running goals. Then make this pact with your coach or someone close to you. Refer to *A Sample Pact* on the next page for ideas of what to include in your pact.

A Sample Pact

I will strive to follow the training program outlined by my coach and contribute to building team unity and spirit. Specifically, I will:

1. Study the scriptures every morning for 20 minutes. Pray every morning and night.
2. Live the Honor Code and do my duty in my church calling.
3. Be on time and ready to run at every team practice.
4. Lift weights twice per week.
5. Take time to warm up, cool down, and stretch properly in conjunction with harder workouts.
6. Encourage others to run well during practices and at meets.
7. Eat three nutritious meals each day.
8. Drink water throughout each day, consciously stopping at drinking fountains every hour or two.
9. Get 7-8 hours of sleep each night preceding a school day or meet, getting to bed no later than 11:00 p.m.
10. Keep current with homework assignments, not allowing myself to get behind.

My sophomore year I was called to be the Relief Society President in my student ward;[2] I was very humbled and a bit overwhelmed by what I considered to be a big responsibility in addition to running, school work, and a social life. I remember putting my faith in Heavenly Father and trusting the scripture, "Seek ye first the kingdom of God, and his righteousness; and all these things shall be added unto you."[3] I can remember promising Him that I would make my church calling my first priority and trust that he would bless the other areas of my life. I know that he did!

I carried 19 credit hours and got almost all A's, my running improved and I placed 2nd at nationals again, plus I had a great social life with many, many wonderful friends. Putting Heavenly Father first before everything and trusting in His promise taught me that He really can and does bless us **far** beyond our natural abilities.

Diane Wilson Creamer, Ricks College cross-country and track & field, 1993-1995. Finished 2nd in both the 1993 and 1994 NJCAA Cross-Country Championships. Personal best: 5000 meters (17:03.35—Ricks College school record)

—Chapter 6—   *Prepare*

You can't expect to perform your best without preparation. Preparing to race obviously involves practice sessions—workouts—but other factors also significantly affect how well you run on race day. To improve your race results, attend to the following areas and recognize their relationship to running performance:
1. Nutrition
2. Sleep
3. Workouts
4. Relaxation and Visualization Techniques
5. Gear
6. Race Day Preparations
7. Warm-Up

1. Nutrition
There are many approaches to manipulating an athlete's diet to improve performance. However, I have found the simplest approach to be most effective for runners. Eat plenty fruits, vegetables, grains, cereals, and some meats.[1] Combine this diet with drinking plenty of water. Observe these nutritional guidelines to keep yourself healthy and energized throughout the training cycle.

2. Sleep
Regular bedtimes and uptimes are less stressful to the body than an irregular sleep schedule. For college-level athletes, 7-8 hours of sleep nightly is optimal. People past their growth stages, with less intense training schedules, can do fine with less sleep. I discourage long naps in the middle of the day, but 15-30 minute

power naps can do wonders to recharge. Get the sleep you need to recover from the daily stress of life and running.

3. Workouts

Training sessions should incorporate activities specific to your running purpose and goals. Follow a plan that allows you to gradually adapt to training stimuli and improve over time. Give yourself enough time to recover from a hard workout so that your energy stores are replenished, your muscles are recovered, and your mind is fresh and alert for racing.

4. Relaxation and Visualization Techniques

To help relax the body and mind, lie down in a comfortable place. Close your eyes and visualize a peaceful location, then alternately tense and relax muscle groups in the body from head to toe. Then visualize yourself succeeding in an upcoming race to program the mind to focus on actions you can take to race better. Try relaxing and visualizing a few hours or a day before your next race.

5. Gear

Wear and bring the proper gear to warm up and race in. Double- check in advance to ensure you have all the necessary running gear and that it's functional. Have spikes (with correct size spikes already screwed in), socks, flats, singlet or shirt, shorts, warm-ups, tape, water bottle, etc. ready to go before beginning to warm up.

6. Race Day Preparations

Try to maintain your normal lifestyle as much as possible while still preparing to race. If you can arise at close to your normal uptime and still have plenty of time to eat and digest a pre-race meal, do it. If you can study, do the wash, read a book or other productive low-energy activity, do it. Spending the whole day thinking about the race can be energy-draining and counter-productive. Drink good amounts of water, but not an overabundance. I have seen good runners bonk in the heat from drinking too much plain water. Condition your body for the race by often doing things you anticipate doing on race day. Then come race day, do things in those ways that you've already rehearsed.

7. Warm Up

Your warm-up's primary focus is to get your body physically ready to race. Your race strategy may need to be fine-tuned here and there, but it should not pre-occupy your thoughts. (It should have been figured out beforehand.) Your self-talk should remain neutral or positive. Any negative thought must be immediately recognized, thrown out, and replaced with a positive one. Following is a typical warm-up plan for a distance race:

Become familiar with the course or track. Review course maps (cross country and road races), observe terrain, locate toilet facilities, and locate your starting position. Get your race number and pin it on shirt or singlet. Jog easy over a section of the course for 5-15 minutes. Do dynamic flexibility exercises for 3-5 minutes. Do build-up strides: 2-3 x 10-20 seconds with full recovery. Do static stretching, if necessary, to loosen any tight muscles. Use toilet facilities. Go to starting area 10 minutes before start. After a few minutes of easy running, run from the starting alley 150-300 meters; run the pace you anticipate starting at. Put on any remaining racing gear, including spikes. Stay in your warm-ups unless the air is warm. Three or four minutes before the start, begin at your starting position, and do 2-4 x 30-50m build-up strides, jogging back to the starting line after each one. One minute before the start, remove your warm-ups, stay loose, and be at your starting position. If the start is delayed, move around to stay loose. Do another build-up stride if the start is delayed more than two minutes.

Write down your warm-up routine.

Write down what you will do to be better prepared at the starting line of your next race.

A lot of the time running for me was about managing pain, and something I learned that helped was to know that I had done everything I could to prepare to race. Sometimes I didn't really feel that getting out of a warm bed before sunrise and running in windy, sub-freezing temperatures on icy Rexburg roads by myself would really help me all that much. When I did it though, I knew I had the mind set to do anything else, because doing just about anything else was a lot easier. That ability to go run in poor conditions made  it easier to run well later in the year at the national championships where a snow storm hit the morning of the race.

Jeff Davidson, Ricks College cross-country and track & field, 2000-2001. Led team to national cross-country championships both years, winning the individual title in 2000 in the cold and snow of Levelland, Texas. Personal best: 3000-meter steeplechase (9:07)

—Chapter 7— # *Practice*

That which we persist in doing becomes easier for us to do; not that the nature of the thing itself is changed, but that our power to do is increased.[1]

To prepare for key races, incorporate into your preparatory races elements you anticipate encountering in those key races.

When deciding each year which races to include in our Ricks College season schedule, I considered what it would be like to race in the regional and national meets and sought to find races that would prepare us for those experiences. For example, the national meet usually has a fairly large number of teams competing, a big- meet feel with loud, up-beat music blaring over loudspeakers, and lots of runners starting out at a faster-than-normal pace. To prepare our teams for such an atmosphere, I always included at least one big invitational meet in our schedule. That way, our teams got the experience of preparing for and racing in a big-meet atmosphere, so it wasn't so foreign to them come time for nationals.

If the regional meet—the qualifying meet for nationals—was expected to be challenging (and most often it was), I tried to schedule a meet earlier in the season on the same or a similar course. If our team or individual runners wanted to experiment with an unfamiliar race strategy, they did so in one of the less important races. If the experiment went well, they felt comfortable about implementing it in the future. If the race didn't go so well, they used a more tested and proven race strategy in the key race.

If you have to travel to participate in a race, the unfamiliarity could upset your preparation for and ability to race. The best you can do in this situation is keep your preparation pattern as normal as possible, or at least make the same changes each time you travel. For example, if you can, observe the same sleep and eating schedules, eat the same types of foods, and drink as much (or perhaps more) water.

The more experience the Ricks College teams got that was similar to our upcoming key races, the better prepared and more successful we were. The same holds true for you as you prepare.

In addition to preparing for key races by practicing in less important ones, you will be better prepared for any race by incorporating certain elements of the approaching racing experience into your workouts. For example, if you wish to run a certain pace in a race, you ought to do some running at that pace beforehand. If you are going to race in hot weather, you ought to do some hard and easy running in hot weather. If you are going to race in running spikes, you ought to do some training in running spikes. If you are going to race with your feet taped, you ought to do some running in practice with your feet taped. If you are going to race barefooted, you ought to do some easy and hard training in your bare feet.

Some take this specificity of training principle too literally and think they ought to practice at a hard race pace everyday. Don't you make that mistake. Your body needs time to recover from the hard workouts, usually between 36-48 hours for a college-age runner. Repeatedly breaking down muscle fibers by repeating hard workouts before the fibers have recovered is a surefire recipe for injury, illness, and staleness. Gradually increasing the muscle fibers' workload to the level they will experience in a big race and allowing them sufficient time to rest, recover, and become stronger is a much wiser plan of attack. In so doing, your muscles and nervous system will stay fresh and invigorated as they anticipate the next workout.

Have you researched the conditions of your next key race? Do so, then write down what you will practice to better prepare for this race

My first year at BYU, I had the chance to run a 10k at Stanford. I wasn´t sure what to expect or how the race would go. When the race started, I began thinking about how 25 laps seemed like a really long time. After a couple laps though, I began thinking about a practice our team had done where we ran 25x400-meters on a target 10k pace. I knew I had completed this practice, so I could run this race at that pace, too. Since there is plenty of time to think in those 10k races, I let myself visualize the practice and imag-  ined each race lap as a 400 repeat. Before I knew it the race was over and I completed the pace I had hit in practice. I know prac- tices give you the strength to run races, but for me they also give me the confidence and mental strength to race at a better level.

Kristen Ogden, Ricks College cross-country and track & field, 1999-2001. Led Ricks team to national cross-country champi- onships both years, winning the individual title in 2000. Per- sonal best: 10,000 meters (33:35.83)

—Chapter 8— **_Perform_**

Take action—a key ingredient to success. Planning and thinking about what you will do is good and necessary. But it is not enough. You will see no results until you execute the plan.

While a freshman at Brigham Young University in Provo, Utah, I trained the first two weeks of practice with about thirty-five other students hoping to make the cross-country team. I frequently found myself among the slower runners, usually in the bottom ten. After two weeks of training together, Coach Sherald James had us run a time trial to determine the top seven runners, who would represent the team at the first meet the following weekend in San Diego. I remember starting out in my usual position near the back of the pack. After the first mile, I began to pass some of the slower runners. With each person I passed I gained more confidence and determination to keep working to pass the next runner in front of me. By the time I reached the finish line, I was in 9th place. I surprised myself and many others by coming out of nowhere to finish so well. A few minutes later, Coach told me that two of the runners who finished before me were academically ineligible to compete; that made me the 7th runner on the team...I was going to San Diego! Doing well in that time trial instilled in me the confidence to run competitively at the college level, which I did, placing among the team's top seven most of my freshman year.

We have all listened to people who talk about the awesome amount of work they plan to put in to become great athletes. But how many actually follow through? Once you have a plan, you need to execute. You need to do the work. Know that it will not be easy. Know that obstacles will arise and tempt you to put off your training until later. Do not procrastinate. Do what you plan to do when you plan to do it. Yes, there are times when you may need to adjust your plan to heal or prevent an injury. But if you procrastinate now, or rationalize that, "missing just this once won't hurt," know you are sabotaging yourself and your future. You must take action. There are times in your training when you need to race, not just practice. A race can help you improve and learn more than merely working out.

Write down the date, time, and place of your next race.

I find that I fear disappointing myself more than I fear the pain of racing. Yes, racing hurts, but the hurt and the pain are temporary; the joy of achieving my goal far outweighs the sting of the journey. I try to begin each race knowing that I am going to succeed because I know I'm going to give my all. I'm confident in my training. I know that I'm prepared. I don't fear failure because I know how to succeed. And as I get more successful races under my belt, racing becomes easier. In my mind I can say, "I have done it before, I can do it again." I rely on my past success to fuel my future determination to keep succeeding. Over time, success becomes a habit, just like brushing my teeth.

Jana Cooke Staheli, Ricks College cross-country and track & field, 1993-1995. Personal best: 5000 meters (18:31.2)

—Chapter 9—   *Pray*

Pray. Express appreciation to God for your many blessings. Pray to be made equal to the task at hand. Include expressions of praise, love, and respect. Acknowledge His hand in your success. Realize that in and of yourself, *you are nothing; as to your strength you are weak; but in God's strength you can do all things.*[1] Seek strength, comfort, and counsel from Him. By humbly seeking God in prayer, you invite Him to bless you in powerful ways.

Search diligently, pray always [in good times and bad]*, and be believing, and all things shall work together for your good.*[2]

Prayer was a natural part of what our students did at Ricks College. These were not memorized or rote rituals, but heartfelt expressions of love, respect, and gratitude to God for their many blessings and talents. Prayers were petitions to be strengthened individually and unified as a team.

We often prayed together as a team in meetings on campus and as we traveled to races. It became a tradition for everyone to gather together before each race for a team prayer. These prayers invited a greater spirit of unity among team members. They eased the anxieties of many, prompting them to relax and keep in perspective what they were about to do. At times, the prayers invited positive thoughts and feelings into the minds and hearts of the athletes, instilling within them the desire to run with greater determination and diligence.

I have found that if your purpose for running includes glorifying God, then you certainly can involve Him in your running pursuits. And if you are striving to do His will, He will be there to strengthen you. As the Lord told Eli in the Old Testament, *"for them that honour me I will honour."*[3]

How could you benefit from prayer?

I learned to really pray when I started to compete my second year at college. I wanted to do well, and I knew that I had the potential. I wasn't sure if my Father in Heaven really cared about running, but I knew that He cared about me and that He had some lessons for me to learn. At the beginning of the season, I prayed to my Heavenly Father and told Him of my desires for success. I also told Him I would do anything He wanted to accomplish the goals I had set. I would work hard and do everything in my power. Throughout that season, I continued to pray and strive to achieve my goals. I had a very successful season: our team won the national championship, and I took 8th place. As great as that was, the greatest achievement was growing closer to my Heavenly Father and knowing He would help me throughout my life.

Jason Brown, Ricks College cross-country and track & field, 1997-1999. Finished second for the Vikings on the 1999 national champions cross-country team in 25:09 over the 8,000-meter course.

—Chapter 10—   *Pfaith*

With a running purpose in harmony with your life's purpose, armed with a solid plan for realizing that purpose, and having made a commitment or pact to follow through, you can exercise faith that as you execute your plan you will progress toward and achieve your purposeful goals.

What is faith? "Now faith is the assurance of things hoped for, the evidence of things not seen."[1] Faith is the motivating cause of all action.[2] When you have faith that your training plan will empower you to achieve your goals, then you will follow your plan. When you have faith in your coach, you'll enthusiastically do what he or she asks you to do. When you have faith in your own abilities, you'll battle through the challenges to be successful. If you lack faith in your training plan, coach, or self, you'll be filled with doubt which will inhibit your taking the action necessary to succeed.

When striving to achieve a goal, you must first believe you can achieve it. You must have a desire to reach it; it must be something you really want—not just a standard that someone else set for you or some abstract wish. You got to *know* what you want and that *you* want it.[3]

With a definite understanding of what you want, and the desire and the belief to achieve it, the following can serve to increase your faith:

1. Observe, visit, or train with others who have already experienced success following a similar plan.
2. Study and learn success principles, pondering how you can apply them to race better.

3. Receive positive, sincere feedback from your coach, training companions, or others whom you respect.
4. As you begin to follow your plan, recognize measurable improvements in your performance, your ability to recover, and how you feel.
5. As you ponder and apply success principles to your running, if they are true principles, you will begin to feel within yourself that they are good; they will enlarge your soul, enlighten your understanding, and "taste" good.[4]

For your actions to reap the benefits of faith, they must be founded on truth. This is why it's important for you to learn correct principles and apply them to your training. If after a period of training you are not progressing as you anticipated, take time to evaluate why. Ask yourself the following questions:

1. Is the training program based on correct principles?
2. Is the training specific to my goals?
3. Does the training program address my specific talent and fitness level?
4. Am I consistently doing the training?
5. Am I confident in my training, my coach, and myself?
6. Am I healthy and balanced in other areas of my life?

If you can answer "yes" to each of the above questions, then you may need to exercise more patience, persisting a little longer to harvest the fruits of your labors. If you answer "no" or "I'm not sure" to any of the above questions, this may give you insight into what you should change. The more you understand correct principles of running success, and the more you apply them with faith, the more quickly you'll become a better runner.

Do you act with faith in following your training plan? What can you do to increase your faith in it?

At the beginning of my freshman year, I remember writing
down my dream goal for the
final race of the season.
This is what I wrote:

MY LADY VIKING DREAM
The 1995 NJCAA National
Championships
Alfred, New York, November
11, 1995 @ 9 a.m.

"Runners, Set!. . ."

In the split second before the
gun goes off and the final race
of my freshman season begins, I
take time to reflect. I think back over the last 5 months and am
filled with assurance that everything will be all right because I
have prepared myself well. It is this moment that I have disci-
plined myself for. I have given my all in every practice—
whether for the team or for myself—competed my hardest in
every meet, eaten nutritionally, and gotten plenty of rest, all to
prepare myself physically. Positive thinking, a winning attitude, past successes, and more have aided in my mental preparation and given me the courage and assurance I need. But,
most importantly, I have prepared myself spiritually. I have
included my Heavenly Father in every workout and performance. And now that I have put forth my best effort, I can put
my trust in Him, for I know that He will direct my paths for
good. I know that there is nothing that my Heavenly Father and
I can't handle together. I am excited and ready for this race.

"Good Luck Lady Vikings! Here we go. . . BANG!!"

As I've thought back to my time at Ricks I realize something significant happened to me as a runner: I didn't just get faster or get in better shape, I gained an inner confidence in my abilities that made my entire outlook on running and racing different. No longer did I approach each race with trepidation, fear, or sheer dread as I had in high school. Instead, I felt eager, excited, and even impatient to do it all again. I truly believe this is because Coach Stutz helped us prepare in every possible way, providing us with an undeniable confidence that only some unforeseen catastrophe could interfere with our capabilities. The power of preparation and faith is real and I believe it makes all of the difference.

Holly Peterson Steed, Ricks College cross-country and track & field, 1995-97. National junior college champion at 10,000-meters in 1996 and 1997. Personal best: 10,000 meters (37:52.46)

Part II:

Race-
Present
P's

—Chapter 11—   *Pace*

As a senior at Brigham Young University, I was surprised to discover that not all runners have as a goal to run their fastest. At the 1985 Wisconsin Cross-Country Classic, our team was matched with six other top teams in the country. I remember coming through the first mile close to 4:50 with only a couple of other runners trailing me and the leaders beyond my sight. I anticipated running the slightly downhill first mile in 4:35-4:40, so I realized I needed to pick up the pace immediately to get back to where I thought I should be.

The next two miles, I did just that, passing runner after runner over the more difficult uphill terrain while keeping my pace in the 4:40-4:45 per mile range. As I was about 400 meters shy of the 3-mile mark, I spied the lead pack just 50 meters in front of me. I continued at my strong pace, catching them just as we reached the 3-mile mark and the large crowd of spectators. Not used to being with elite runners at this stage of a race, I thought I would do well to stay with them and let them help pull me along.

As I joined their pack, I had to slow down to stay with them. I was surprised. At the 3-mile mark of a big important race, the lead runners were content to jog along together. I was stunned when they continued to plod along for another 120 meters. Their breathing was easy, very relaxed…too relaxed. I thought to myself, "This is crazy!" As a middle-of-the-pack runner I had never once thought of taking it easy in the middle of a race. What should I do? How much longer would they continue jogging along before taking off at a blistering pace to the finish? I knew I couldn't match the speed of these elite runners, so I decided to take action. I moved out from my position behind this front pack and resumed my normal race pace, surging to the front. No sooner had I made my move than everyone else in the group took off and blew past me, throwing elbows and expressing their displeasure at my forcing them to start racing again so soon. I never caught up to these runners again, but I finished with a faster time and a higher place than ever before in a meet of that caliber.

If your goal is to run a fast time, what pace should you run throughout the race? Should you start fast, hoping to give yourself enough of a cushion to make up for your fatigue later in the race? Should you start slow, gradually picking up the pace, so you can finish with a big sprint at the end? Or should you run the same pace the entire distance?

To run your fastest, consider Newton's Laws of Motion expressed in the mathematical formula F=ma (Force = mass x acceleration). This formula teaches us that force must be applied to an object for it to accelerate. However, because of inertia, no force is required to maintain a constant speed (in the absence of resistance). When the resistance is constant, it requires less energy to maintain the same speed than it does to speed up or slow down. Applied to running this means **you run most economically when running at an even pace over the entire distance**.

This is a key concept in pacing that many inexperienced runners fail to grasp. Many young runners want to start out fast, thinking their best chance of winning or running a fast time is from a position in the front. What they fail to realize is that running too fast early in the race leads to oxygen debt and a premature build-up of lactic acid in the muscles, resulting in early fatigue. Following such a practice may result in victory in short races or against inferior competition, but the longer the race or the more talented the competition, the more pronounced the consequences of this error.

You run most efficiently by maintaining a consistent pace throughout the race. If you are like most runners, this means you must start slower than normal; the pace must feel very comfortable. During the first part of distance races, you ought to be able to talk without undue effort. Don't expect this easy, comfortable feeling to last forever...it won't. The farther you get into a race, the more discomfort and fatigue increase. (Focus on other Ps to help you delay and deal with these feelings while still maintaining your pace.) Focusing on this P—running an even-pace race—will get you further into a race still feeling comfortable and strong. Once you understand the wisdom of running even-pace races and put that strategy into practice, you will achieve faster times and higher place finishes.

How do you determine your even pace? Simply divide your goal finish time for the race by the distance in miles. The result will be your average per-mile pace. This is the pace you will run from start to finish to achieve your goal time. Include some running at this pace in your training to get a better feel for it.

If you have never tried running an even-pace race, anticipate a race-time improvement of 1%-2%. It's less risky to try to run a race time just slightly faster than you have run recently than to try to aim for a time that is significantly faster. Follow King Mosiah's counsel to do all things "in wisdom and order; for it is not requisite that a man should run faster than he has strength."[1] Often, runners who try to make a big time jump from one race to the next overextend themselves early, hastening the onset of fatigue, and fail to attain their lofty goals. In fact, they often end up running worse than they had previously. Such negative results often pile up, crushing the confidence of the once optimistic runner. A more moderate approach more often leads to positive, confidence-building results.

Maintaining a consistent pace on a track is easy to monitor; the distance of each race segment is known and is consistent in elevation gain and loss (none) and in terrain (same track surface all the way around the track). Monitoring the evenness of your pace on a cross-country course may not be as simple. The elevation gain and loss over different segments of the race may vary quite a bit. Also, the running surface may change from one segment to the next, or even several times within one segment. The effort required to run one mile on pavement varies significantly from that required to run a mile on thick, slick grass, or on sand or gravel. Because of the inconsistency, it's also difficult to measure even-pace running on inconsistent terrain. Therefore, it's a good idea for you to do some training on consistent surfaces to develop a feel for what even-pace running feels like. That way, when you do run on inconsistent terrain, you will be able to gauge your effort and match it to the feel of a consistent pace, even if your actual pace varies.

Before the race, divide the course into smaller segments (for distance races of 5 kilometers or more, a mile is a good segment size to use). For each segment, set an acceptable pace range. The faster end of this range represents the fastest you are willing to run to be in an acceptable position during that stage of the race. The slower end of this range represents the slowest you are willing to run to be satisfied with your position and target finish time. Your target range should be fairly narrow—usually no more than 10 seconds per mile. Remember, if your goal is to run a fast race, run very close to even pace throughout the race. Do not jeopardize your ability to do that by running either too fast or too slow at the start.

Most races have an official who reads off times as you finish each lap on the track or as you come by the first mile of an off-track race. However, if you want to make sure you receive accurate times to help you assess your pace, you should wear a watch with a stopwatch function or have a trusted friend stand at each mile mark to read your time as you pass by.

If you come through the initial stage in the position you want and within the target time, continue to run the race as planned. If you come through faster than your target time, you may want to consider easing up a bit to get back on pace. However, be careful not to ease up too much. Remember, running an even-pace race does not mean running an even-pain one. The first mile will usually feel quite comfortable and easy. You can expect this ease and comfort to fade away as you exert increased effort and endure greater pain, maintaining the same strong pace further into the race. If you come through the first stage slower than your target time, you'll probably want to pick it up a little to reach your target pace.

When adjusting your pace, aim to run the next segment at the target time; do not try to get your cumulative time back to where you initially planned it to be. If you do, you will accelerate or decelerate too much and find yourself off-pace going into the following segment of the race. In the long-run, this will end up costing you valuable energy.

In summary, if your goal is to run fast, you should strive to run an even-pace race. To do this, you:
1. Divide your goal finish time by the number of miles in the race. This is your even pace per mile.
2. Include some training at this pace.
3. Divide the race into smaller segments (for example, in one-mile increments). Determine a target time range for the first segment.
4. While maintaining a desired position with respect to the other runners, run comfortably, aiming to pass the first segment mark within the target time range.
5. If your time at the first segment mark is outside your target time range, adjust your pace to run the next segment in your target pace time range.
6. Continue running each segment at a consistent, even pace.

There may be races where you want to get out from the starting line very quickly, at almost a sprint. This type of strategy is usually dictated by a very large field of runners on a course that narrows or has a sharp turn very early in the race. However, I would not recommend you use this strategy unless you have successfully experimented with it in practice. If you know one of your most important races will dictate using a faster start, you should prepare by doing interval workouts that mimic this scenario. (For example, when doing 1200m intervals, run the first 200 meters four-to-six seconds faster than your 5km race pace, then finish the remaining 1000 meters at your normal 5km race pace.) Start fast when maintaining the next P—Position—is a higher priority than maintaining an even pace.

After determining the pace you want to run, how accurate are you in running at that pace? How do you gauge your accuracy? What will you do to improve your feel for pace?

What is your goal finishing time for your next race? What is the average per-mile pace to achieve that time? What is the target pace range you want to run for the first mile of your next race? What is the per-mile pace for each of the subsequent miles in the race?

Excerpt from personal journal dated Saturday, September 11, 1999:

Today I ran my very first race as a member of the Ricks College cross-country team. During the long bus ride to Bozeman Montana, Coach took time to interview each of us individually. He asked us what our goals were for this particular race. I told him that my personal goal was to run an even-paced race. Pace had been on my mind since our team meeting yesterday, when coach taught us "A  Plethora of P's for Phenomenal Performance." It was hard at first to keep a consistent pace because soon after the gun went off, everyone passed me. I had to fight back my pride as I found myself in the very back of the racing pack. Rather than letting myself get discouraged, I simply focused on keeping my pace steady and staying relaxed as Coach taught me. I eventually began to pass people one at a time, using another one of Coach's strategies, "passing with power" as I moved up in the pack to eventually finish 28th out of 58 runners. I was excited about how I ran and was pleased that I had met my goal of running an even-paced race.

Holly Campbell Yorgason, Ricks College cross-country 1999. Personal best: 3-miles (19:25)

—Chapter 12—   *Position*

Before your next race, decide which place you hope to finish in. Then decide what position you should to be in in each stage of the race to finish in that position.

Throughout the race, be aware of your position with respect to the other runners; usually you will want to run close to runners with similar abilities. However, keep pace in mind while focusing on position, because there is little value in starting fast if you are unable to maintain a strong pace.[1]

If you do not know others in the race with similar ability, focus more on pace during the initial segments. Once you establish a position, focus on maintaining or improving your position as the race progresses.

Be aware of your relative position with respect to other runners throughout the race. Some aspects to focus on include your position with respect to:

1. *The entire field of runners.* How many runners are in the race and what is your current position among them?
2. *The leaders.* How much distance or time is there between you and the leader?
3. *Team members.* Who and how many of your teammates are between you and the leader? How many teammates are between you and the back of the pack? Is this relative position where you expect to be? If not, what will you do about it?
4. *Other competitors.* The same questions you ask yourself regarding your position among your teammates could be asked regarding your position with respect to other competitors.

Being in good position also means running the course in an energy-efficient manner. Hug the inside on corners to run as short as distance as possible. However, be willing to run the extra distance on someone's outside shoulder through the turn if this will enhance your overall position or help you run a more even pace.

Running just behind someone is less taxing than leading the pack. From behind, you can also better observe how those in the pack are doing. However, running in a pack increases the risk of getting caught in pack congestion, hindering your freedom to run how and where you want. This disadvantage is more pronounced when the pack is larger or when the course is narrower.

In what place do you hope to finish in your next race? In what position with respect to other runners do you expect to be in after getting settled into your pace? How will your pace and that of the other runners affect your position?

Position is everything! I remember at Ricks we had a motto: "Unity is power." We would always run as a pack for the first part of the race, known as the pack attack. By running in this position, we were able to draw strength from each other and push each other to keep going. I remember Regionals in 2000, when I felt weaker than usual and not as strong mentally. By running with a teammate and not letting her out of my sight, I was able to hold a position until I felt strong enough to push it harder.

The synergy of running in a group always gave me greater strength and I know it's one of the reasons that year's team was able to accomplish what we did: we learned to work with each other and achieve more together.

Kristen Ogden, Ricks College cross-country and track & field, 1999-2001. Led Ricks team to national cross-country championships both years, winning the individual title in 2000. Personal best: 10,000 meters (33:35.83)

—Chapter 13—   *People*

Your primary focus should be on racing people, not the clock. This is true even if one of your goals for the race is to run a fast time. Racing people usually brings out the best in your performance because it is not uncommon in cross-country or road races for the marked distances to be inaccurately measured. If you base how fast you are running by what the clock says as you pass the marked one-mile point, and that mark is in reality 20, 50, or even 100 meters off, you may end up adjusting your pace based on inaccurate feedback. Other factors such as challenging terrain, wind, and clock inaccuracies can also lead to split times that are misleading.

If you go out in a race and get yourself in a good position with respect to other key competitors and to the entire field, chances are you are running at a good pace even though a clock or a mile marker may tell you otherwise. And if the clock happens to be correct after all, and your pace is a little bit off, you'll know everyone else is probably off in their race plan just as much as you are. If your focus is racing people you will finish in a good position.

Your running is stronger and more relaxed when you run with other runners. By running next to other runners, you can draw on their energy and their cadence to pull you along without having to focus on your own resources. Running in a group usually provides significant mental and physical conservation of energy.

After establishing your position, every time you pass another runner, your mind congratulates yourself and tells you, "Way to go! You are strong! Keep it up! You can go get the next one!" Draw on this positive reinforcement to gain strength and renew your determination to continue on. On the flip side, feelings of doubt and fatigue can creep into your mind every time you get passed. When you get passed after establishing a position, you should ask yourself, "Am I still running at a good pace? Am I in good position to achieve my race goal?" If you can sincerely and confidently answer "yes," then there's no need to alter your race plan. But if your answer is "maybe," "I don't know," or "no," then try going after or running with someone in front of you. If you are unable to do so, you probably ran the first part of the race too fast.

Write down how you will focus on people in your next race.

One of the greatest lessons I learned at Ricks College was the value of running smart. I always had much more success-ful races where I didn't let the excitement of the race get to me. I would start slower than most, at a pace that I knew I could maintain. As the race went on, other runners would start to tire, and I would pass them. Each person I passed would boost my confidence. The last 800 meters is where I would start to pour it on, little by little. This would get me ready for the 200-meter sprint at  the end where I don't believe that anyone has ever passed me. I always felt like I had given it my all in races that I ran this way.

Amasa Mecham, Ricks College cross-country and track & field, 1998-99. Ran to a 5th place finish in the 1999 NJCAA 3000-meter steeplechase final. Personal best: steeplechase (9:32.18)

—Chapter 14— *Pform*

Focus on technique cues throughout the race to improve your running economy—in other words, run your fastest while using your energy most efficiently.

Strive to develop a running style that maximizes your running economy. Focus on moving forward faster while using as little energy as possible. This is best achieved when muscles are supple, flexible, strong, well-coordinated, and trained for the proper balance of speed and endurance as needed for your event.

Focus on the following technique cues as you run. A good way to begin learning these techniques is to run 40-50m build-up strides while focusing on one cue at a time. As you perform each stride, evaluate your technique for that particular cue. It is helpful to have a coach or runner observe and give feedback. After doing a few strides while focusing on one cue, move to the next cue. Continue this process until you have gone through all the cues.

Technique Cues

Run Tall: Imagine you are a horse on a merry-go-round. You are anchored in position by a pole, which keeps your head, torso, and hips all in line, centered over each other. The pole keeps your head focused straight ahead—it can't move up and down or side to side. The pole keeps your head centered squarely over your torso. The pole keeps your torso centered squarely over your hips. So as you run, Run Tall like a merry-go-round horse with a pole keeping your head, torso, and hips all in line and centered over each other. Run Tall!

Brook Trout: Before beginning this cue, make the scariest face you can and hold it for 5 seconds. Relax your face for a few seconds, and then repeat making a scary face. Relax again. As you repeat this one final time, focus on what happens to your jaw, face, and neck as you relax. What happens? Your jaw drops, and your mouth hangs loosely open. Because the jaw relaxes, the rest of your face and neck muscles also relax. When you picture a Brook Trout, see its big jaw just hanging there. When the trout works hard, it doesn't grit its teeth or screw up its face; its jaw just hangs there. So as you run—whether you're running fast, moderate, or slow—remember the Brook Trout with its jaw dropped and mouth hung loosely open. Brook Trout!

Shoulders Down: Before performing this cue, make your shoulders as tight as possible, and hold them there for five seconds. Relax your shoulders for a few seconds before tightening them a second time. Relax again. As you repeat this one final time, focus on what happens to your shoulders as they relax. They should relax and drop down. (Depending on how you held them, they also went forward, back or just straight down.) As you run, ask yourself, "Are my Shoulders Down?" Shoulders Down!

Shoulders Wavy: When using the Shoulders Down cue, don't *hold* your shoulders down. Instead, there should be a very slight up-and-down movement of the shoulders as you run. When you run, your shoulders should oscillate like a very small sine wave. As you run, ask yourself, "Are my shoulders loose and oscillating like a small sine wave?" Shoulders Wavy!

Light Hands: Before addressing this cue, make as tight a fist as you can with each of your hands for five seconds. Relax your hands and drop them to your sides for a few seconds, then repeat. Do this a third time. Then, while keeping your hands at your sides, and without moving your fingers or wrists, ask yourself, "What do my fingers and hands look like right now, when they are in a relaxed position?" You will notice your fingers are in a slightly curved position and that the tip of your thumb and the tip of your index finger are almost touching. You will also notice there is space between your thumb and your palm, allowing **light** to pass through. This is how your fingers and hands should look as you run!

Some distance runners run with the tips of their fingers touching the palm of their hand. While some can run that way and stay fairly relaxed, others tend to curl their fingers more tightly against their palms as their running intensifies. This is especially true of sprinters. This is why you often see sprinters run with flat palms and their fingers fully extended—they want to avoid making fists as they press for maximum speed. They know that tight hands lead to tightness throughout the upper body, which is counterproductive.

As you run, remember to keep your hands and fingers in a natural, relaxed position. Light Hands!

Thumbs Up: Here's another exercise to demonstrate the purpose for this cue. Hold your hands out in front of your body with the elbows flexed at a 90-degree angle. Face the palms of your hands toward each other. Now rotate your wrists, so your palms face up. Now rotate them back 180 degrees, so the palms face down.

As you rotate the wrists back to the "palms up" position, notice what happens to the elbows: they are drawn in toward your torso. Now notice what happens to the elbows as you rotate the wrists back again to the "palms down" position: they are drawn out away from your torso. Ask yourself, "Which position is more energy efficient: elbows in or elbows out?"

If you answered, "elbows in," you are correct. So does that mean you should run with your palms up all the time? No! Remember which way the palms of your hands face when they are totally relaxed. But it does mean you want to avoid running with your palms in the "palms down" position. To help you remember to keep your hands in a "palms in" position, think Thumbs Up. This does not mean that you literally want to have your thumbs sticking up as you run...you don't. But if you did, would your thumbs be pointing up or pointing in? If you drew straight lines from each of your thumbs to the heavens, would those two lines be parallel or would they intersect? As you run, ask yourself, "Are my hands positioned to keep my elbows close to my torso? If my thumbs were sticking up, would they be pointing straight up or in a little?" Thumbs Up!

Chest High/Hip Pocket: What should your arms' range of motion be as a distance runner? As your arm swings forward, your hand should raise to somewhere between your navel and chest. As your arm swings backward, it should reach your hip pocket. As you race, the range of motion for your arms should be from Chest High in the front to Hip Pocket in the back. Chest High/Hip Pocket! Note: When running faster than this pace (for example when sprinting), the range of motion increases in both the forward and backward arm swings. The key is to keep the motion as smooth as possible while coordinating the actions of the arms with those of the legs.

Arms Forward, Straight Ahead: As your arms swing forward, they'll naturally come across the torso somewhat to counteract hip rotation. However, your arms should not come so far across the torso that they contribute additional unwanted rotation. In the forward arm swing, no part of the hand should cross or even touch the mid-line of the torso. You should direct your arms forward and straight ahead. Arms Forward, Straight Ahead!

No Robots: Although Arms Forward, Straight Ahead is an important cue, remember that your arms need to come across the torso somewhat to counteract hip rotation. If they were to literally swing straight back and forth like a robot, they would not generate the counter-rotation necessary to keep the body moving forward efficiently. No Robots!

All Five Toes: As you push off the ground with your foot, focus on pointing the foot forward rather than in or out. If you naturally underpronate by coming off only the little toes on the outside of your foot, or if you naturally overpronate by coming off only the big toe, recruit the muscles in your other toes to add more power to your push-off. All Five Toes!

Turnover Up: Some runners tend to overstride; in effect, they put on the brakes slightly every time a foot lands. To help correct this weakness, try the following test: Run for 60 seconds, counting the number of strides you take (for example, count every time your left foot contacts the ground). Repeat this test several times, running at various speeds. If your turnover count, or rate, is between 90 and 100, your stride length is probably close to what it should be.[1] If your rate is less than 90, you are likely overstriding.

Focus on increasing your turnover rate to 90. You may think about shortening your stride length a little, but this will likely happen naturally if you simply focus on increasing your turnover. If your turnover rate is higher than 100, you are probably understriding. (Either that, or you are sprinting.) If this is the case, then focus on pushing more forcefully off the ground with each foot strike. Don't focus on reaching out with your foot while it is in the air in hopes of making your stride longer. Evaluate your stride turnover frequently as you run. Work to keep your turnover up at all times when you are running. Turnover Up!

Note: Taller runners generally have a more difficult time achieving a turnover rate as high as 90. In fact, tallest runners usually have the slowest stride rates. This does not mean that tall runners should abandon increasing their turnover toward 90; as the gap shrinks between their turnover rate and the goal of 90, their efficiency will noticeably improve.

After you have done a few sessions practicing these cues, you will begin to feel more comfortable with the technical improvements you are seeking. Then you will be equipped to cycle through the cues one-by-one as you run, doing a self-check to see if you are performing each cue correctly and energy-efficiently. A complete self-check can eventually be done in a matter of seconds. Repeat the self-check often throughout the run to spot technique areas which need attention. Recognizing and correcting your flaws can get you back running correctly, economically, and on the fly.

Very Important Note: Correcting poor running form requires you to take a long-term perspective; it won't happen in a day, a week, or sometimes even a month. Initially, running efficiency may decrease as you try something foreign to your running template (what you are used to). But if you really want to become a more efficient runner, are committed to focusing on these cues frequently, and are willing to work on them long enough to make them natural, you will become more efficient. Focus on the cues while doing speed work, while doing long runs, while doing tempo runs, and while doing strides. The more you work on the cues, the sooner you will feel comfortable and smooth using correct form.

Another Note: Realize that some individuals have anatomical or biomechanical abnormalities which keep them from incorporating these cues into their running technique. They should not feel pressured to practice them or feel inferior because their technique does not match that described above.

Decide when you will focus on your form. How will having better form help you race better?

Throughout my freshman season at Ricks, I focused on running with good form. After the first 2.5 miles of the NJCAA cross-country championship race, I felt pain start to creep in and my body start to tire. Instead of focusing on overcoming the pain, I concentrated on maintaining my form. I told myself to relax and went through the checklist of form cues. As I focused on my mechanics, I felt more relaxed and filled with power and energy. By concentrating on my form I felt the time pass quickly, and I found the finish line drawing closer.

I leaned into one final big hill, focusing on moving my arms and legs and keeping my body relaxed. In no time, I was at the top of the hill and continuing on to the finish line. I felt a rush of adrenaline in response to the cheering crowd. As I began my final sprint to the finish, those familiar friends, pain and exhaustion, visited me yet again. Focusing on smooth arm movement, relaxing my mouth and jaw, and keeping my hands loose, I moved even faster as I approached the finish line. Never before had I focused so intently on my form throughout the final two miles of a race. I finished in a personal best time.

Ever since, I have continually focused on my form in my workouts and races. Not only do I feel better when I use good form, but I perform better.

Andy Robinson, Ricks College cross-country and track & field, 1999-2000. Personal best: 8000 meters (26:13)

—Chapter 15—   *Pfocus*

Focus to learn and adapt more quickly to change. Engage yourself in performing rather than just going through the motions.

As you gain practice and race experience, you will learn what to focus on while you race. Staying focused keeps you "in" the race. "Zoning out" may cause you to forget your purpose and plans for the race, stopping you from quickly responding to challenges. Staying focused keeps you so engaged in the race that the time seems to fly right by. Many of our Ricks College runners, on the eve of running a 10,000 meter race on the track for the first time, were apprehensive about how long and boring 25 laps was going to be. But as they raced and focused on appropriate cues, they got caught up in the thrill of racing and never gave boredom a chance; the 25 laps seemed to pass in a moment.

At any given moment, you can focus your attention on only one thing. While many people appear to multi-task, what they really do is focus their attention on one item for a short period of time, then abruptly shift their attention to a second item, then shift again to a third item or back to the original. This process of focusing and shifting focus enables you to process a lot of relevant information in very small packets of time. It keeps your mind and body alert and ready to respond. Using this ability to focus and refocus quickly, call up "P" cues in your mind at appropriate intervals throughout the race to keep you on course with your running plan. Cycle through all the technique cues to check yourself for proper technique and relaxation. Repeat this cycle to help you maintain proper form throughout the race, especially when you begin to feel tense.

What will you focus on in preparing for and running your next race?

It isn't uncommon for races to be held in less than desirable weather, and for the longest time I'd let that affect me. In my sophomore year at the national cross-country championships, I was complaining about the snow. Coach Stutz told me I shouldn't be thinking about the cold and snow during my race; that I should be too busy focusing on my running. So I tried it. I just focused on running, and I don't ever remember feeling the cold and snow that day.

Courtney Allen Riding, Ricks College cross-country and track & field, 1999-2001. Personal best: 1500 meters (4:43.05)

—Chapter 16—   # *Persist through the Pain*

When you experience non-injury pain, it doesn't mean it's time to slow down or quit. Rather, it is time to persist to achieve new levels of performance.

In 2000, Angie Benson was recruited to Ricks College as a hurdler. I invited her to join our cross-country team that fall to strengthen her training base for spring track. For a newcomer to the sport, Angie did well, but finished behind our top seven runners, failing to earn a spot on the team that went to the national championship meet.

In track, Angie experienced a frustrating season as a 400-meter hurdler; she usually ran faster than a teammate in practices, but never beat her in a race. When she asked me about it, I told Angie that her teammate was more determined to win, pushed through the pain, and fought to the end.

When Angie returned to Ricks College for her sophomore cross-country season, she was bent on improving so she could go to Nationals with the team. She determined to seek the strength of the Lord, persevere through the pain, and fight to the end. She said, "Each workout was a new opportunity to reach the point where I had to either give in to the pain or push through it. I strove to persevere through the pain and keep going strong."

In her first race, she surprised everyone by finishing third for the team. She realized her hard work and determination were paying off, so she worked even harder. By the time Nationals arrived, Angie was our team's top runner. Here is her description of the national championship race and her reflections on her sophomore season:

"We ran together as a team the first mile. It was awesome to be in a pack consisting of my teammates, empowering one another as we ran. After the first mile, we began to spread out and I pushed ahead with a couple of my other teammates. In the middle of the race I could feel the fatigue starting to come. I knew I had to keep pushing. As I approached the biggest hill in the course, there were still a few girls ahead of me. I pushed hard up the hill to catch one girl; coming over and down the hill, I passed another. There was now only one girl and one small hill ahead of me. I worked hard up the hill and came around the corner. The girl was just ahead of me with only about 500 meters left to go. I felt the fatigue course through my body, and I wondered if I would be able to pass the girl with power, keep the pace, and stay in front of her. I had to make a decision: give in to the pain and doubt, or keep fighting to the end. I knew it was time to dig deep and give it all I had. I said a prayer in my heart and ran my hardest. I passed the girl with as much power as I could muster, and then gave it all I had. It was painful, but I willed my body to push through it and win the race. What a cool feeling that was! I had not only accomplished my goal to compete in the National race, but I had won it!

"I still remember that feeling. I know I was helped and strengthened throughout the race, and when I had given all I could, I felt an extra push. My thoughts quickly turned to what President Bednar had taught us about the enabling power of the Atonement, and to the running principles Coach Stutz had taught us. I was experiencing the fruits of my efforts of living after these principles.

"I learned valuable lessons that year: I learned that if we set goals, exercise faith that the Lord will help us reach them, and persevere through whatever barrier may arise, we can accomplish those goals. Each trial we face gives us the opportunity to choose to persevere with faith in the Lord. As we do so, we can overcome the trial, becoming stronger because of it.

"If I had not worked hard and pushed through the pain in my earlier races, I would not have been strong enough to push through the pain to win the National race. It takes practice and persistent efforts to reach our goals."

Non-injury pain is temporary. You feel it when you run fast for an extended period of time, allowing lactic acid to accumulate in your muscles. Give yourself time to stop and catch your breath, and the pain subsides. Obviously, you can't stop and take a break during your race without losing ground. However, you can condition yourself to persist throught the pain longer than you may think.

As your muscles begin to accumulate large amounts of lactic acid, they send messages to your brain that your body cannot continue running at its current pace. Instead of giving in, tell yourself that you can keep working hard, thereby convincing your body to continue just a little bit longer.

Are you willing to persist through the pain?

Note: Before attempting to **Persist through the Pain** or **Partition** (next chapter), you should receive a physician's clearance to run intensely. You should be in good physical condition, having already completed a solid base of conditioning. When you sense pain associated with injury, you'll have to decide if continuing to run hard is worth the risk of greater damage. If breathing becomes unusually difficult or your body temperature feels unusually hot, stop running immediately and find someone who can assist and observe you until your breathing and body temperature return to normal.

I do several things to persist through the pain. I have found that concentrating on keeping the pace really helps me ignore the pain, while concentrating on form and relaxation helps me maintain a strong pace. I also have little tools that help me through speed work sessions. I like to count or do math. Counting to fifty as fast as I can, as many times as I can, helps me survive many speed workouts. And in a race, concentrating on the people ahead of me helps keep my mind off of the physical pain.

When I was at Ricks College, I would always choose to run the 10,000-meter and the 5,000-meter races at the national track & field championships. The problem is that the events were only one day apart. I cannot begin to describe what it feels like to try and race again the day after a 10,000m. Your legs feel like lead. But I found that if I just concentrated on running one lap and didn't worry about the next lap, I could make it to the end of the race. Sometimes I would even have to talk out loud to myself, just to keep my mind off the fact that my legs were so tired they couldn't move. It worked; two different years I was an All-American in both the 10,000m and the 5,000m.

Malia Steiner Kinghorn, Ricks College cross-country and track & field, 1991-1994. Personal best: 5000 meters (17:19.80, 2nd fastest in the history of Ricks College)

—Chapter 17—

Partition

Partition the race into smaller, less intimidating pieces. Concentrate on one small segment at a time. When you break up the race and focus on one piece at a time, you extend your ability to perform at a high level.

A few years ago while visiting my parents in Utah, I went for an early Saturday morning run and discovered that a 5k race would be held in town later that morning. I decided to enter. When I arrived at the starting line, I discovered two of my former BYU teammates, Timo Mostert and Jerry Henley, were running as well. Though it had been about fifteen years since we had raced together, we were all still in decent running shape—Jerry was even a sponsored runner for a local business. Back at BYU, we each had our races when we ran faster that the others, but more often than not, I ran the fastest of the three. As we lined up on the starting line now fifteen years later, even though there were another two hundred plus runners in the race, we could sense that for us, this really boiled down to a three-man race.

As the race started, my two former teammates and about a dozen other athletes bolted to the lead. I went out faster than I had planned just so I could stay somewhat in contact with them—I was about ten meters behind Timo and another ten meters behind Jerry at the one-mile mark. I thought, "These guys are in pretty good shape. This is going to be a challenge." By the 1.5-mile mark, Timo and I were running together, still about twenty meters behind Jerry and a couple others who trailed the two leaders by a growing distance. As we ran together, it was obvious I was breathing noticeably harder than Timo. This race was hurting me more than it was him, and we both knew it.

At two miles, the pace continued fast. Timo and I were both beginning to feel the lactic acid accumulating in our legs, but neither of us was going to let the other go, nor did we want to give up on catching Jerry. At 2.4 miles, Jerry and his small pack began to slow slightly. I told myself, "I just have to catch Jerry." By 2.5 miles, I passed Jerry and his group and set my sights on the second place runner, who was about fifty meters ahead. Jerry did his best to come with me and Timo fought to catch Jerry. My legs were burning, but I wasn't about to let myself ease up. With four street blocks to go, I kept telling myself, "Just make it to the end of the next block." I repeated this each time I finished one block and began the next. I felt like I was flying the last four hundred meters to the finish. It wasn't enough to catch the young highschooler ahead of me, but it was enough to lengthen the distance between myself and Jerry and Timo. As I crossed the finish line, I was thrilled to have run a great race and to have finished in front of my old teammates one more time. Glancing at my watch, I also realized my time was the fastest I had run in several years.

Too often runners concentrate on how much longer they have to run and how much it hurts. Often they slow down, thinking it might help them recover and make one last dramatic kick to the finish. But no matter how impressive their kick might be, it won't make up for what they lost by slackening the pace and losing contact with other runners.

What do you do when lactic acid builds up in your muscles and you start to feel the burn? Answer: Persist through the Pain. How? Partition. Break the rest of the race into small pieces, and focus on maintaining the pace and/or keeping pace with another runner for just one segment at a time. Find something stationary along the course that you can reach without slowing your pace, then maintain your pace until you reach that marker. Don't think about what you will do after you pass that physical marker. Just focus on getting there.

You are placing a partition in your mind to keep from thinking any farther ahead. As you reach that marker, congratulate yourself and pick out another marker a short way ahead. Then keep your pace until you reach that marker. Again, don't worry about how you are going to maintain your pace any further than to the next marker. Once you reach that marker, continue partitioning and following through to each marker until you finish the race. You may have to reduce the distance between markers as you get further into the race. That's okay. Just keep going. It's amazing how much farther you can run at a good pace by following this tactic.

Note: Since partitioning can stress your leg muscles more than they are used to, be sure to take extra care to recover following the race. This includes a cool-down walk or jog, light stretching, and icing the legs. Massaging the legs with ice cubes or an ice cup two or three times per day for two or three days following the race can help reduce the recovery time.

How will you partition the race in your mind the next time you begin to feel the urge to slow down?

Partitioning the Race

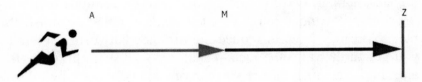

When most runners start to feel fatigue in a race (point M), they think about how much farther they have yet to run to reach the finish (point Z) and believe they can't possibly maintain their pace that much farther.

When you start to feel fatigue (point M), find a landmark (point T) you believe you can reach without slowing your pace. In your mind, set a partition at point T and don't let yourself think past that point. Make your sole focus maintaining your pace to that point.

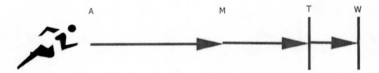

When you reach point T, immediately find a new landmark (point W) you believe you can reach without slowing your pace. Once again, set a partition in your mind at point W, and don't let yourself think past that point.

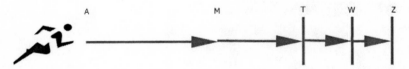

Continue partitioning the race into manageable segments until you cross the finish line (point Z).

It was a beautiful and crisp autumn morning in Richmond, Virginia, and I was excited to run my first marathon. I had been told by several veteran marathon runners that no matter how well you prepared yourself for the race, nothing could prepare you for the pain and mental breakdown you would suffer during the last six miles. I did not realize how right they were until I reached mile 20. Fatigue had set in, my toes were badly blistered and my quads were on fire. Every step was increasingly painful. I was physically

breaking down, and I knew that to finish this race I needed to remain mentally tough. I told myself, "only one more mile to the finish line." I reached mile 21, and again I repeated to myself, "only one more mile." I passed miles 22, 23, 24, repeating the phrase over and over in my mind. Finally, I reached mile 25. "Only one more mile," I whispered to myself. When the finish line came into view, I was overcome with emotion. Nothing could stop me now.

Melody Sheppard Jenson, Ricks College cross-country and track & field, 1997-1999. Personal best: 1500 meters (4:45.13)

—Chapter 18— *Pass! (Pass with Punctuation)*

Pass other runners decisively. This communicates to them and to you that you are strong and capable of maintaining your faster pace.

Passing other runners confidently gives you immediate positive feedback: you are running at a stronger pace. It inspires you to continue pressing forward with renewed determination. It pumps up your belief that you can continue running strong.

Recently, I joined a handful of BYU-Idaho cross-country runners attempting to run under five minutes for a mile on the track. After running the first two laps in 76 and 75 seconds, respectively, another runner and I drew close to a slowing runner coming out of the first turn on the third lap.

As I moved up on his outside shoulder, he picked up the pace to try to keep me from passing him. We continued running side by side as we approached the turn past the half-way mark of the lap. Not wanting to run the extra distance staying on his outside shoulder through the turn would require, I tucked in close behind him. No sooner did we enter the turn than he slowed the pace. Knowing we would not stay under five minutes if we slacked off the pace now, I reacted immediately, moving out and around him in a matter of seconds. I was back in the inside lane before I reached the middle of the turn.

I continued the steady pace, coming through the third lap in 74 seconds. The runner I had passed and the other I had been running with for two-and-a-half laps were two seconds behind. I knew we were hurting, but I also knew we all could break five minutes if we ran tough during the final lap. I picked up the pace slightly for the next 300 meters, stretching the gap between us to three seconds with 100 meters to go. At that point, I dug even deeper to find another gear—and so did the two runners behind me. I crossed the finish line in 4:56; the other two crossed in 4:58. All of us were elated to have achieved our goal—a feat none us probably would have achieved that day if I hadn't passed them decisively when I did.

When you plan to run an even-paced race, it's likely you will pass other runners as the race progresses. Those who start out fast and then slow down, find it hard to keep up with a passing runner. Keeping your pace even will, in most cases, be sufficient to pass slowing runners decisively. However, slowing runners with some fight left may pick up the pace as you try to pass. When they do, stay with them—maintain your strong pace. Once you feel them start to slow the pace just a little, make your move—pass them with power.

Sometimes in a race you and other runners may match each other almost stride for stride. When you feel it is time to move past them, accelerate and make a decisive move. This decisive move can steel your resolution to keep a strong pace to the finish. Failing to move decisively, may emboldened your competition to stay with you and then outkick you at the finish. Why give them the chance? If you pass decisively, you can create a large enough gap to render ineffective any kick they might have left? Don't just think "pass" when approaching or passing another runner, but "Pass!" That is, Pass with Punctuation.

How will passing others decisively help you race better?

Passing with Punctuation was always my favorite thing to do. When I got ready to pass someone, I'd take a few deep breaths, so the competition wouldn't hear me breathing hard. Then, as I went from right next to them to just in front of them, I'd plant my foot extra hard and imagine leaving an exclamation point in the dirt. It always made me feel good to pass someone, and even better to pass with punctuation!

Kelly Johnson Nielsen, Ricks College cross-country and track & field, 1995-1997. Personal best: 3000 meters (10:29.27)

—Chapter 19— *Positive Self-Talk*

"As a man thinketh in his heart, so is he."[1] Positive thoughts give you the confidence to perform better.

I remember the 2000 National Junior College Cross-Country Championships held in Levelland, Texas. (The city was appropriately named—the course was the flattest I've ever seen for a national cross-country championship.) For the second Saturday in November, everyone figured the temperatures would be mild, if not a bit too warm for racing. However, the morning of the race, we awoke to cold wind and rain that turned to snow before race time. Many of the teams and runners present murmured about having to race under such conditions. But our Ricks College team members got excited. Why? Many said, "This is just like running in Rexburg in the winter time." Though some of the freshmen had not yet experienced a Rexburg winter, they bought into their teammates' enthusiasm.

Running in the snow, on icy grass, and through mucky mud, our Lady Vikings battled strong, coming out as team champions. Kristen Ogden, a sophomore from Chico, California, who was among our top three runners throughout the year, came across the finish line ten seconds in front of the nearest competitor to capture the individual honors—her best race ever.

In the men's race that followed, our Vikings surprised the competition by storming to a convincing victory. Individually, Jeff Davidson, a freshman from Burley, Idaho, came from behind to beat a strong field of runners by ten seconds. His five mile time of 25:53 may have been the slowest winning time for a national championship meet, but under the conditions, it represented a great effort—his best. The two days previous to the meet, Jeff had been sick and unable to train or do much of anything else with the team. Although he arose the morning of the championships feeling much better, not many believed he could keep pace with the more talented athletes in the field. After the first mile it may have looked that way, as Jeff ran with the rest of our team's lead runners, ten seconds behind the lead pack. But the race was going just as Jeff envisioned. He told himself he was feeling strong and in good position. By the three-mile mark he had worked his way up to the lead pack, passing them near the four-mile mark and pushing on to an uncontested victory. Jeff Davidson, Kristen Ogden, and all of our team members took what easily could have been a negative situation and turned it into a positive one just by what they decided to think and feel about it.

There are two keys parts to positive self-talk:

1. State your thoughts as positive affirmations. For example: "I feel strong," or "I am prepared to run well," or "This is going to be a great challenge and opportunity."

2. Exercise faith in that positive affirmation. As was discussed in the chapter on Faith, exercising faith means taking confident action on a true belief. Believe the positive affirmation you make, and do all you can to bring it about.

Be careful to state a positive affirmation you believe in. Stating an affirmation you have no faith in can be counterproductive. When it does not lead you to greater achievement, you begin to question the statement's validity when, in truth, it is your lack of belief that undermines the desired improvement.

If you think negative thoughts about your performance, your chances of success are slim to none. Conversely, if you think positive thoughts and exercise faith in them, your ability to succeed will increase dramatically.

When competing and thinking about your performance, are your thoughts usually positive or negative? The next time you start to think negatively about your performance, what will you do to refocus on the positive things you are doing and can do?

As a mid-distance runner, cross-country was something I tolerated in order to be in shape when spring came and I could hit the track. At least this is what I told myself. I think I really just didn't know how to run cross-country well. Come race day, I would start the race strong with my teammates, but after a mile or so it would hit me—that winded, rubbery-legged, tired, hurting feeling. As I felt this come on, my mind typically spiraled into a panic of negative thoughts. In turn, my breathing became more labored, slowing my pace, which resulted in my being passed by other runners. This prompted another cycle of negativity until it was all I could do to finish the race.

And then it happened. It was during a cross-country race towards the end of my collegiate running career. The gun went off, and as I began running, I began to talk to myself internally. I told myself over and over again that I was okay, that I was doing fine. Suddenly the first mile was done...how strange. It had gone by so quickly, and I still felt pretty good. I continued to talk it out in my mind, and slowly everything seemed to fade away—I could no longer hear the bystanders cheering or feel the burning that usually seared my lungs by this point in the race. Time seemed to slow down, yet the miles were melting away so quickly. And suddenly I was done! Even more exciting was that I had placed really well, and I felt great, like I could go run it all over again. It was then I realized I had finally gotten into "the zone" during a cross-country race. My positive self-talk had given my mind mastery over my body, allowing me to push myself beyond what I ever thought possible.

Melanie Clark Steere, Ricks College cross-country and track & field, 1996-1998. Helped team to 1997 national junior college track & field championship by winning the 800-meter race in 2:11.78. Personal best: 800 meters (2:03.40)

—Chapter 20— *Pick it up at the End*

No matter how you've run when you're near the end, accelerate to the finish.

Stand near the finish line of almost any distance race, and you will see runners crossing the finish line at a pace much faster than their normal race pace. Why and how are they running so much faster in the closing meters of the race? Maybe it's because:

1. They know the race is just about over. They can take an extended rest to recover afterwards. The pain of running hard will be temporary and the satisfaction of having given their all will last a lifetime.

2. They know they still have untapped energy reserves left. In tandem with the muscle fibers and energy sources already in use, additional muscle fibers and energy reserves can create a burst of speed for a short-term, high intensity effort at the end of a race.

3. Those runners are better sprinters than other distance runners. Some are born with a greater capacity for speed. Others have trained themselves to run fast even when fatigued. Add some short, fast intervals at the end of hard workouts to improve your ability to pick up your pace at the finish.

4. They feel great, having reserved too much energy by running too easily earlier in the race. If you ever find yourself with too much energy near the end of a race, enjoy your sprint to the finish. However, after the race is over, realize that even though you may have passed a lot of people as you kicked to the finish, your time and place would have been better if you had been tougher mentally and run a faster pace throughout the race.

5. The runners are responding to the crowd at the finish line cheering them on. More people tend to stand, watch, and cheer at the finish line. Racing in front of a crowd and hearing them get excited for you can raise your adrenaline level.

How about you? Do you usually finish a race with a strong closing kick? If so, how and why are you able to do so? What is your motivation—what empowers you to do so? Whatever it is, know this: You can pick up the pace and finish strong at the end of any race, regardless of how you may have run the race up to that point. Unless racing rigor mortis has set in, you can always find additional physical reserves to pick up the pace for a final kick to the finish. Knowing this, you should never consider the possibility of slowing down or easing up earlier in the race just to conserve energy for a spectacular, eye-catching kick at the finish. Your goal should be to run a strong, consistent race all the way through, then add a kick somewhere near the finish.

As you plan the next race, decide in advance where you will begin your kick. Write down what you will tell yourself as you begin your kick and continue strong through the finish line.

It was my sophomore year at Ricks, and the NJCAA Track and Field Championships were in Kansas. Adrenaline, excitement, nervousness—every emotion possible flooded my body as I prepared for and began to run the 3000 meter race. My goal of becoming an All-American in track was on the line. With little over a lap left in the race, my teammate and I were battling over 5th and 6th place. We had run a hard pace and were exhausted. Trying to muster up enough energy to finish strong, I was reminded  of something Coach often told us: "No matter how fast you run a race, you can always pick it up at the end." I picked up my pace and took command of 5th place. I passed the fourth place runner with punctuation, making sure she knew I wasn't quitting there. Rounding the last corner, I took over third place, where I finished strong. I brought home the bronze medal and was named third team All-American. Even though I had given my all during the first six laps of the race, I was still able to pick it up at the end and run about as fast on my last lap as on my first.

Katie Williams Marshall, Ricks College cross-country and track & field, 1996-1998. Personal best: 3000 meters (10:22.29)

Part III:

Post-Race P's

—Chapter 21— **Praise**

Give credit to those who are instrumental in helping you to succeed.

Those to praise following a race:

1. Yourself
2. Close competitors
3. Teammates
4. Coach
5. Meet officials
6. Meet director
7. Supporters
8. God

1. Yourself. You did it! You took the risk to extend yourself beyond your comfort zone. You saw how running and racing could help you achieve your purposes in life and followed through on your commitment to act and achieve. You battled through the challenges of a race, learning things along the way that will help you to be even more successful in the future. Congratulations for having *"fought the good fight, for having finished the course, for having kept the faith."*[1]

2. Close competitors. You know you can run much better when someone else is running close by you, helping to pull and push you along. Competitors don't need to be viewed as enemies. It is much healthier to view competitors as those who stretch you to your limits, who draw out your best efforts, who test you so you become the best you can be. Express appreciation to those who run near you during the race, both those you finish in front of and those who finish in front of you.

3. Teammates. If you are part of a team, you have teammates who have spent countless hours training with you in an effort to race well as a team. During the race some of these same teammates may run along side you and/or encourage you as you run. Don't forget to thank these people for the significant impact they have on your running experience.

4. Coach. Ideally, your coach understands your purposes and goals, your plan for achieving them, the effort you put into running, and has counseled you, encouraged you, comforted you, challenged you, and inspired you along the way. Even if you don't agree with everything your coach says or does, praise your coach for the time he or she spends trying to help you and your team become more successful.

5. Meet officials. These are the people who make the race run as smoothly as possible. They make sure you are entered in the race, that you know where to run, that you can run safely, that you receive an accurate finishing time and place, that you receive drinks during longer races and refreshments afterwards, and a multitude of other duties, so you can relax and have a great experience. Nearly all meet officials give their time and effort without any financial compensation. Without them, the race would not happen. Go out of your way to thank these people before and after any race you are involved with.

As a side note, if you are not planning to run in an upcoming race in your community, consider volunteering to serve as a race official.

6. Meet Director. This is the person responsible for all the details that go into a successful event. The meet director decides what elements to include to make the event inviting to runners and the supporting community. If you have a good experience, be sure to voice your appreciation. If you have a suggestion of how to improve the event, the meet director is the person you should contact.

7. Supporters. People don't usually watch a race for entertainment like they do football and basketball games. You know if they come to watch and cheer it's because they know and care about a competitor. If that competitor is you, be sure to let your supporters know how much you appreciate their encouragement.

8. God. There are many who do not have the physical abilities that you do. Know that your body and talents are gifts from a loving Heavenly Father—gifts you possess now, but who knows for how much longer. Develop these precious gifts while you can. Acknowledge God's hand in all that you are able to accomplish.

There is something ennobling and empowering in praising others. It demonstrates humility. It acknowledges the contributions of others—many others—in helping you become who and what you are. By praising others, you invite them to continue sharing themselves with you, which will help you improve even more.

Write down a list of those you will remember to praise following your next race.

Through my years of running, some of my best friends were my fiercest competitors. Even after struggling against each other throughout a race, we would always hug and congratulate each other afterwards. We would be sure to say "thank you" and tell one another that we couldn't have done it without the other pushing us the whole way.

Cindy Reeder Fowers, Ricks College cross-country and track & field, 1988-1990. Led team to national junior college cross-country championship in 1988 & 1989. Won the 1500-meter race at the 1990 NJCAA track & field championships. Personal best: 1500 meters (4:32.57)

—Chapter 22— *Pause to Ponder*

Take time out to evaluate your progress and fine-tune your plan. Taking an occasional break can help you refocus and replenish energy reserves. Evaluate how well you are achieving your purpose for running.

Most all the meets our Ricks College cross-country teams participated in were quite a distance away. Usually that meant a 3-hour-or-more bus ride back to Rexburg following the meet. After we took some time to get something to eat and talk about the team performances, I would often have the students write down three things they felt they did well that week and in the race, and then three things they learned or needed to improve on. Then, one by one, each would visit with me about these reflections. If a runner had not run too well, it was sometimes difficult to come up with three positive observations about the performance. But with a little prodding, everyone could eventually come up with three positive statements about their individual accomplishments. Even if the student ran strong consistently, that student would continue to write down things learned as well as things to improve on. These counseling sessions, following periods of personal reflection by the athletes, were some of the most powerful learning experiences we shared together.

I feel it is critical that runners honestly list some positive things about themselves and their performances, whether they have met their running goals or not. As an athlete, your confidence in your running abilities is positively linked to performance, and that link is often fragile. An athlete who consistently puts him or herself down usually performs consistently worse.

Always find something positive about yourself and your performance, and then build from there to improve.

Most of what you learn comes from taking the time to pause and reflect upon your experiences, and then articulating your feelings more clearly by writing them down. Sharing these learning experiences implants what you learned deeper into your soul.

From your most recent race, write down three things you did well and three things you learned or will improve on. Reflect upon how well you are achieving your purposes for running. Share your observations with someone close to you.

After many track meets, I remember boarding the bus for an unappealing long ride home. I didn't look forward to the ride because all the distractions kept me for using the time efficiently; however, one thing that I came to anticipate and appreciate was the one-on-one meeting with Coach Stutz. He always used this travel time to talk with each athlete individually. If we raced at home and there was no traveling involved, he would schedule meetings in his office the following Monday. In each of these meetings I  had the opportunity to pause and think about my most recent performance. Evaluating my performance and determining whether I was making progress towards accomplishing my goals became a very important tool for me. Stopping to pause and ponder helped me to remain focused on long-term goals, learn from my mistakes, and refocus if necessary.

Brick Bergeson, Ricks College cross-country and track & field, 1995-1996, 1998-1999. Personal Bests: 1500 meters (3:42.7); 800 meters (1:48.39)

—Chapter 23—   *Press Forward*

After doing a positive performance review, move on to the next step of your plan. Don't dwell on past mistakes or poor performances. Press forward.

Just about everyone has a less-than-successful race at one time or another. Illness, stress, unforeseen obstacles, confusion about the course, slacking in commitment, or other factors diminish performance. When you fail to accomplish the degree of success you anticipate in racing, your reaction to that failure will largely determine how quickly you bounce back to achieve success in the future. After taking time to reflect, make a positive plan for the next time you run. If you need to repent of any bad habits, do so. Learn from your mistakes, weaknesses, and inexperience, then move on. There is no benefit in continually beating yourself up, so repent and get over it. I have seen too many runners—good runners—who fail in one race and start thinking of themselves as losers or blaming others for their own shortcomings. If runners continue to dwell on these negative feelings, so much fear of failure builds up by the next race that they perform even worse. Don't let your disappointment and fear snowball; change and move on. If you come home from a race feeling discouraged with your performance, analyze your performance, seek counsel from your coach, make necessary corrections, and take action to perform better from that point forward. Learn from the past. Put it behind you. Look forward with faith to the future. This is the quickest and surest way to get back on course and press forward.

On the flip side of this coin are those who become filled with pride when they succeed. If initial success came easily, without a great deal of effort and sacrifice, they may seek only quick and painless solutions to their future challenges and not become converted to practicing success principles. They may become wise in their own eyes and fail to seek or give heed to counsel from wise coaches. If you experience great, even unexpected success, be wise. Don't become filled with pride and emptied of gratitude. Follow your plan and learn from the experience to continue achieving success in the future. Praise others, acknowledge your blessings, and press forward.

After each race (whether you consider it to be a resounding success or not), pause to evaluate it, learn from it, set your sights on being successful in the future, and then move in that direction.

How will you press forward full of faith and free of fear or pride?

As a walk-on at Ricks College, I finished 5th in tryouts for the varsity cross-country team. I was elated. My running improved over the next two weeks, and at our first meet I finished 3rd on the team and 9th overall. I could not have been more pleased. However, as school became more demanding and practices more intense, I hit a slump. My practice performance suffered, and at the next two meets I finished 8th on the team. Afterwards I recorded the following in my journal: "I felt like I just could not run fast. I  think part of it was worrying and having a fear in the back of my head that I would not perform as well as I did at our first-meet. Still, I feel terrible; I really don't know how to handle it."

I was extremely discouraged, not to mention embarrassed, in front of my new teammates and coaches. Soon thereafter, Coach Sonderegger related to our team how he felt when learning that his eleven-year-old son had cancer. That day I recorded the following in my journal: "Coach told us today that he and his wife felt scared, worried, and sick inside considering that they might lose their son. But then he realized that those types of feelings do not come from Christ; they come from Satan, who tries to discourage us in times of trial. Christ gives us feelings of comfort and peace." Although my trial paled in comparison to what my coach was experiencing, his comments helped me realize my feelings of fear, worry, and discouragement did not come from God. I needed to make an emotional and psychological adjustment. I resolved to quit dwelling on my negative feelings and focus on the next practice, the next meet—one run at a time. I also told my coach how I felt. We examined my workout schedule and concluded to cut back on my morning runs. The changes paid off, and I again ran competitively in practice. At our region championship meet, I felt confident, fresh, and relaxed. I ran well and finished 3rd on the team. I rode that momentum into track season, where I finished 2nd in the 5,000m and 3,000m steeplechase at our region track & field championships.

Matt Dixon, Ricks College cross-country and track & field, 1990-1991. Personal best: 3000 meter steeplechase (9:36)

—Chapter 24— *Put it all Together*

Integrate the P's into your running program to consistently run your best.

Now that you've read through The Plethora of P's, you may be asking yourself, "How can I best implement this into my running program?" The answer to that question is probably best answered by you and your coach.

If you are like most runners, you are implementing one or more of the P's in your running and racing already. You may not have been consciously aware of them, but now that you are, you can focus on them to hone your abilities and consistently perform better.

You may be tempted to focus on all of the P's the very next time you race. However commendable that ambition may be, you will reap better results by focusing on just a few P's at first. Remember, learning occurs "line upon line, precept upon precept."[1] As you prepare to train, race, or analyze your performance, refer to the questions found at the end of each chapter that pertains to the P's you choose to focus on. Answering those questions will help you evaluate your effectiveness in implementing those P's to be successful. (A complete list of the P's and their accompanying self-analysis questions are located in the Appendix. You may wish to make a copy of this list for yourself to use for each race you run.)

After you become adept and comfortable implementing a few P's, you can add a few more to your repertoire. With practice and experience you can eventually become skilled at implementing all the P's. The more you practice, the more natural it will become, and the greater the success you will accomplish in your racing.

Hundreds of runners have implemented the Plethora of P's into their racing with greater, more consistent success as a result. Will you be next? When will you begin?

Coach, as I was thinking of memories to share, I thought how much running and your Plethora of P's has impacted me as a person. I learned that with a plan and the right amount of preparation anything is possible. I graduated with high honors from college. I am happily a mother of two beautiful girls. It takes a lot of persistence, because life deals us some bad hands, but with prayer and faith I always seem to put it all together. These concepts have taught me to never do things half-way and to always be the best I can, both in running and in life.

Katie Williams Marshall, Ricks College cross-country and track & field, 1996-1998.   Personal best: 3000 meters (10:22.29)

Appendix: Key Questions for
Implementing *Race Your Best*

Purpose
What are your purposes for running? Which purpose is most important to you?

What's your purpose for your next race?

Purposeful Goals
Based on your purpose for running, what are your goals for the season or year?

Based on your purpose, what are your goals for your next race?

Plan
What's your long-term plan to achieve your running purposes and goals?

What will you do to prepare for your next race?

What strategy will you use in your next race?

Price
What commitment and sacrifices are you willing to make to achieve your running purposes?

What will you commit to do in order to be successful in your next race?

Pact
What pacts will you make to achieve your running goals? With whom will you make these pacts?

Prepare
What is your warm-up routine? What will you do to be better prepared at the starting line of your next race?

Practice
Have you researched the conditions of your next key race? What will you practice in training to better prepare for your next key race?

Perform
What are the date, time and place of your next race?

Pray
How could your running benefit from prayer?

Pfaith
Do you act with faith in following your training plan? What can you do to increase your faith in it?

Pace
After determining the pace you want to run, how accurate are you in running at that pace? How do you gauge your accuracy? What will you do to improve your feel for pace?

What is your goal finishing time for your next race? What is the average per-mile pace to achieve that time? What is the target pace range you want to run for the first mile of your next race? What is the per-mile pace for each of the subsequent miles in the race?

Position

In what place do you hope to finish in your next race? In what position with respect to other runners do you expect to be in after getting settled into your pace? How will your pace and that of the other runners affect your position?

People

How will you focus on racing people in your next race?

Pform

Decide when will you focus on your form? How will having better form help you to race better?

Pfocus

What will you focus on in preparing for and running your next race?

Persist Through the Pain

Are you willing to persist through the pain?

Partition

How will you partition the race in your mind the next time you begin to feel the urge to slow down?

Pass! (Pass with Punctuation)

How will passing others decisively help you race better?

Positive Self-Talk

When competing and thinking about your performance, are your thoughts usually positive or negative? The next time you start to think negatively about your performance, what will you do to refocus on the positive things you are doing and can do?

Pick it up at the End

As you plan the next race, decide in advance where you will begin your kick. What will you tell yourself as you begin your kick and continue strong through the finish line?

Praise

Whom will you remember to praise following your next race?

Pause to Ponder

As you ponder your most recent race, what are three things you did well and three things you learned or will improve on? Reflect upon how well you are achieving your purposes for running. Share your observations with someone close to you.

Press Forward

After each race, pause to evaluate it, learn from it, set your sights on being successful in the future, and then move in that direction. How will you press forward full of faith and free of fear or pride?

Put it all Together

What can you focus on now to best implement *Race Your Best* into your running program?

Chapter Notes

Acknowledgements
[1] Alma 26:12 (Book of Mormon: Another Testament of Jesus Christ [BoM]).

Chapter 1: Purpose
[1] David A. Bednar, conversation with Ricks College track & field team, May 1999.
[2] Alma 43:29.
[3] Alma 43:45.
[4] Alma 43:48.
[5] Alma 43:48-50.
[6] Alma 45:1.

Chapter 2: Purposeful Goals
[1] Leslie Householder, The Jackrabbit Factor (Mesa, AZ: ThoughtsAlive, 2005), 165-169.

Chapter 3: Plan
[1] Stephen R. Covey, *Seven Habits of Highly Effective People* (New York: Simon and Schuster, 1989), 95.
[2] David A. Bednar, Brigham Young University-Idaho Athletic Morningside, 9 October 2003.
[3] 2 Tim. 4:7 (New Testament [NT]).
[4] Alma 53:20.
[5] The workout schedule combines my own ideas with those from great coaches' such as Sherald James, Jack Daniels, and Joe Vigil. The pace intensities denoted by the letters E, T, I, and R are from Jack T. Daniels, Daniels' Running Formula, 2nd Ed. (Champaign, IL: Human Kinectics, 2005), 50. The Stepping Stone workouts are from Joe I. Vigil, Road to the Top (Albuquerque, NM: Creative Designs, 1995), 100.

Chapter 4: Price
[1] David A. Bednar, "According to Thy Faith," Ricks College devotional (29 August 2000), 5.
[2] Luke 14:28-30 (NT).
[3] Moroni 10:6-9 (BoM).

Chapter 5: Pact
[1] William H. Murray, The Scottish Himalayan Expedition (London: JM Dent & Sons, 1951).
[2] Relief Society is an church organization for women. Two of its primary objectives are compassionate service and strengthening women. A student ward is a congregation of usually 160-200 students. So Diane's calling to serve as ward Relief Society President gave her stewardship responsibility for the spiritual strength of about 100 single young women.
[3] Matt. 6:33 (NT).

Chapter 6: Prepare

[1] Doctrine and Covenants (D&C), Section 89.

Chapter 7: Practice

[1] attributed to Ralph Waldo Emerson (see www.transcendentalists.com/emerson_quotes.htm).

Chapter 9: Pray

[1] see Alma 26:12.
[2] D&C 90:24.
[3] 1 Sam. 2:30 (Old Testament).

Chapter 10: Pfaith

[1] Hebrews 11:1 (Joseph Smith Translation of the Bible).
[2] Joseph Smith, "Lectures on Faith 1:9-10."
[3] Leslie Householder, 165-169.
[4] See Alma 32:27-28.

Chapter 11: Pace

[1] Mosiah 4:27 (BoM).

Chapter 12: Position

[1] There are situations which warrant a faster than normal start: a)When you think you can improve your chances of winning by creating an early gap between you and the competition, or b)When the course layout demands you establish a good position early because it hinders the opportunity to improve your position later on. This condition is usually created by the course being too narrow too early for the number of competitors.

Chapter 14: Pform

[1] Jack T. Daniels, Daniels' Running Formula, 2nd Ed (Champaign, IL: Human Kinectics, 2005), 93-94.

Chapter 19: Positive Self-Talk

[1] Proverbs 23:7 (OT).

Chapter 21: Praise

[1] see 2 Timothy 4:7 (NT).

Chapter 24: Put It Together

[1] 2 Ne. 28:30 (BoM)

Recommended Books

Clarke, Ron. 1966. *The Unforgiving Minute*. London, England: Pelham Books

Covey, Stephen. 1989. *Seven Habits of Highly Effective People*. New York, NY: Simon and Schuster

Daniels, Jack. 2005. *Daniels' Running Formula*. 2nd Ed. Champaign, IL: Human Kinectics

Green, Larry and Pate, Russ. 2004. *Training for Young Distance Runners*. 2nd Ed. Champaign, IL: Human Kinectics

Householder, Leslie. 2005. *The Jackrabbit Factor*. Mesa, AZ: ThoughtsAlive

Orlick, Terry. 1986. *Psyching for Sport*. Champaign, IL: Leisure Press

Pfitzinger, Pete and Douglas, Scott. 1999. *Road Racing for Serious Runners*. Champaign, IL: Human Kinectics

Vernacchia, Ralph, McGuire, Rick and Cook, David. 1996. *Coaching Mental Excellence*. Portola Valley, CA: Warde Publishers

Vigil, Joe. 1995. *Road to the Top*. Albuquerque, NM: Creative Designs

Wilmore, Jack and Costill, David. 2004. *Physiology of Sport and Exercise*. 3rd Ed. Champaign, IL: Human Kinectics

Wooden, John. 1988. *They Call Me Coach*. New York, NY: McGraw-Hill

Index

About the Author

Doug Stutz ran cross-country and track while attending Brigham Young University in Provo, Utah from 1979-1986. He interrupted his education to serve a two-year church mission in Argentina from 1980-1982. At BYU, he earned a bachelor's degree in business while minoring in sports coaching. He went on to earn a Master of Sport Science degree in sport management from the United States Sports Academy in Daphne, Alabama in 1987.

Stutz arrived at Ricks College, a private two-year college nestled in rural Rexburg, Idaho, in 1987 as an assistant coach in cross country and track and field. His competitive skills and experience combined with his education quickly translated into coaching skills that translated into success for Ricks College runners.

In 1992, Stutz was named head coach of the men's and women's cross country program. Success came immediately and with it, a dynasty in junior college distance running. The men's team showed immediate improvement, placing in the top eight at the national finals on eight occasions, topped by national championships in the final three years of the program in 1999, 2000, and 2001. Doug also coached seventeen young men to All-American status, including 2000 NJCAA champion Jeff Davidson of Burley, Idaho.

The performance of the women's team under Coach Stutz's guidance was remarkable. In 1992 the team took third at the National Junior College Athletic Association championship meet. The Lady Vikings improved to second in 1993 and 1994. Their progress continued, reaching the top spot at the national meet in 1995, then stunning the competition by repeating as NJCAA champions in 1996, 1997, 1998, 1999, 2000, and 2001. During that string, Stutz coached four individual champions, Kara Ormond in 1996, Alycia Boyer in 1998, Kristen Ogden in 2000, and Angie Benson in 2001. The NJCAA acknowledged Doug's success by naming him national Coach of the Year seven times.

Seven times his teams won the award for best combined men's and women's team performances at the NJCAA cross country finals.

When Ricks College became Brigham Young University-Idaho, intercollegiate sports competition was dropped, but Doug stayed on and continues to teach in the Activities Program as the sports advisor for cross country, track & field, and adventure racing. (For more information about the unique BYU-Idaho Activities program, visit activities.byui.edu.)

Doug uses a wholistic approach in training athletes. He emphasizes not only workouts, but also adequate rest, nutrition, and proper mental preparation. He approaches life the same way, whether it be in academics, social, or spiritual activities.

Doug's wife Keysha is a sprinter-turned-distance-runner who ran for Ricks College in 1987-1989. The two live in Rexburg with their seven children.

You may obtain additional copies of *Race Your Best* by visiting RaceYourBest.com on the Internet.

After applying these principles to your own racing experience, you are invited to share your success stories with others on the RaceYourBest.com Web site.

For more information, contact Doug Stutz at the following address:

Doug Stutz
162 K Street
Rexburg, ID 83440
208-313-5606

LaVergne, TN USA
14 September 2010
197031LV00003B/30/P